Praise for *Designin*

"*Designing a Motivational Syllabus* provides practical guidance, but it is much more than a how-to. It presents new ways of thinking about the role of the syllabus. Drawing from current research on best practices, Harrington and Thomas provide thorough context and make a strong case for an effective course syllabus as a foundational tool to shape student learning. This book will undoubtedly be valuable to new and experienced teachers as well as faculty development professionals."—*Billie Bennett Franchini, Interim Director, Institute for Teaching, Learning and Academic Leadership, SUNY Albany*

"This book is a tremendous resource for all faculty, whether you are teaching freshmen introductory courses or advanced graduate courses. It does not matter if you are a novice or an expert professor; this book is a beneficial and useful guide for improving an existing syllabus or designing a new one. Harrington and Thomas demonstrate how a syllabus is much more than an informative document—they show us how it can be a valuable tool to motivate students and assist them in their learning."—*Kathleen F. Gabriel, School of Education, California State University, Chico*

"Designing a syllabus is a task to which faculty often give little thought. However, in this engaging and thoughtful book, the authors have crafted a guide that is both helpful and a teaching tool. The authors weave student learning throughout the book and have developed a resource that will help both new and seasoned faculty. And, because the book is so well written, it is accessible to all, regardless of discipline."—*Chris Hakala, Director, Center for Excellence in Teaching, Learning, and Scholarship; and Professor of Psychology, Springfield College*

"The authors insightfully apply principles from the motivation research literature to demonstrate how course syllabi can be powerful tools for stimulating students' enthusiasm and motivation to actively engage in course activities. While the book is an invaluable resource for designing a syllabus that maps out a path for student success, it also provides information on course design, assessment, and teaching approaches. It is a must-read for all faculty who want to construct a syllabus that is sure to increase student engagement and learning!"—*Saundra McGuire, (Ret) Assistant Vice Chancellor; Professor of Chemistry; and Director Emerita, Center for Academic Success, Louisiana State University*

"In *Designing a Motivational Syllabus* Harrington and Thomas provide compelling rationale and evidence for why instructors would want to reimagine their syllabus, while offering practical advice for how to create a document that accurately articulates their vision, motivates students, and fosters learning. Subtle in their approach, they quite cleverly shift the focus from syllabus creation to course design, and in doing so, signal the importance and seriousness of such work. Instructors, whether wishing to make small changes to their syllabi or to totally rethink the whys and hows of their courses, will find this book an invaluable resource."—**Michael Palmer**, *Director, Center for Teaching Excellence; and Professor, General Faculty, and Lecturer in Chemistry, University of Virginia*

DESIGNING A MOTIVATIONAL SYLLABUS

The Excellent Teacher Series

Series Editor: Todd Zakrajsek

This series offers fresh approaches to teaching and learning by reviewing traditional methods in light of evidence-based strategies to promote practices that best facilitate student learning. Each volume of the series is written to provide early career faculty with specific strategies that can be quickly implemented, midcareer faculty with the opportunity to adapt and expand on what is currently used, and experienced faculty with new perspectives to augment thinking on foundational aspects of teaching and student learning.

Completed titles:

Forthcoming titles:

DESIGNING A MOTIVATIONAL SYLLABUS

Creating a Learning Path for Student Engagement

Christine Harrington and Melissa Thomas

Foreword by Kathleen F. Gabriel

Series Preface by Todd Zakrajsek

STERLING, VIRGINIA

Published by Stylus Publishing, LLC.
22883 Quicksilver Drive
Sterling, Virginia 20166-2019

Library of Congress Cataloging-in-Publication Data
Names: Harrington, Christine, 1971- author. | Thomas, Melissa, 1978- author.
Title: Designing a motivational syllabus : creating a learning path for student engagement / Christine Harrington and Melissa Thomas.
Description: First edition. |
Sterling, Virginia : Stylus Publishing, 2018. |
Includes bibliographical references. |
Identifiers: LCCN 2017049070 (print) |
LCCN 2018001942 (ebook) |
ISBN 9781620366264 (Library networkable e-edition) |
ISBN 9781620366271 (Consumer e-edition) |
ISBN 9781620366240 (cloth : alk. paper) |
ISBN 9781620366257 (pbk. : alk. paper)
Subjects: LCSH: Education, Higher--Curricula--United States. |
Curriculum planning--United States. |
Motivation in education--United States. |
College teaching--United States.
Classification: LCC LB2361.5 (ebook) |
LCC LB2361.5 .H366 2018 (print) |
DDC 370.15/4--dc23
LC record available at https://lccn.loc.gov/2017049070

13-digit ISBN: 978-1-62036-624-0 (cloth)
13-digit ISBN: 978-1-62036-625-7 (paperback)
13-digit ISBN: 978-1-62036-626-4 (library networkable e-edition)
13-digit ISBN: 978-1-62036-627-1 (consumer e-edition)

Printed in the United States of America

All first editions printed on acid-free paper
that meets the American National Standards Institute
Z39-48 Standard.

Bulk Purchases
Quantity discounts are available for use in workshops and for staff development.
Call 1-800-232-0223

First Edition, 2018

*To my faculty colleagues for inspiring me
to improve my teaching practices*
                                    —Christine Harrington

*To my students who push me to be the best
teacher I can be for them*
                                    —Melissa Thomas

CONTENTS

FOREWORD

C HRISTINE HARRINGTON AND MELISSA THOMAS'S book, *Designing a Motivational Syllabus: Creating a Learning Path for Student Engagement*, is a tremendous resource for all faculty, whether you are teaching freshmen introductory courses or advanced graduate courses. It does not matter if you are a novice or an expert professor; this book is a beneficial and useful guide for improving an existing syllabus or designing a new one. Harrington and Thomas demonstrate how a syllabus is much more than an informative document—they show us how it can be a valuable tool to motivate students and assist them in their learning.

In today's college classrooms, our students are more diverse than ever before. As professors, we must reach out and support our students in meeting the challenges and academic rigors of higher education, because student success at our colleges is a vital part of our society and our democratic system. As many of our forefathers noted, having an educated public is a requirement for having a democratic society. As professors, we have a major role in helping students be successful. Each semester, our task begins when we first introduce students to the course syllabus. Harrington and Thomas explain how to create a syllabus that will guide students throughout the semester so they will not only master the learning outcomes of a course but also make academic and social gains that will prepare them for citizenship in a democratic society.

Harrington and Thomas provide guidelines for preparing a clear and explicitly detailed syllabus that will benefit and motivate all the different learners in our classrooms. All types of students—be they honors or academically at-risk—will appreciate a syllabus that is expertly designed, and Harrington and Thomas show us how to accomplish this daunting task. Professors will find many excellent examples on how to highlight the value and purpose of their courses.

When describing the essential components of a syllabus, Harrington and Thomas present options for faculty, such as criteria for informing our students of the crucial and indispensable aspects of the course. The authors also present the research and rationale for the various components that a syllabus should include. By following Harrington and Thomas's advice, we can improve our syllabi in ways that will stimulate students' interest and simultaneously "encourage the feeling of being part of a community at the start of the semester" (p. 46). The authors demonstrate how to use the syllabus as an additional tool for building rapport with students.

Harrington and Thomas understand the dilemma that many of us face in creating a balanced syllabus so that it is not a heavy-handed policy document with a negative tone, but rather a document that promotes professionalism and aligns our policies with our learning goals. They give us excellent ways to shape a syllabus in a positive and inviting way so that students know what is expected from them.

Harrington and Thomas also cover how to use a syllabus to help students grasp the relevancy of a course. They give many different options for setting up and analyzing grading systems and explain how we can clarify our rationale for different assignments to students. Being able to connect all learning activities and assignments to the learning outcomes of the course will increase student motivation and help them be aware of the best ways to learn the content of a class.

Harrington and Thomas have provided not only a step-by-step process for creating a thoughtful and comprehensive syllabus but also tools for self-evaluation and techniques for seeking feedback from students and fellow faculty. The syllabus checklist and rubric examples they provide are excellent ways for helping us improve, expand, and enhance a syllabus so that professors can capture students' attention and respect and, at the same time, offer students support.

In summary, I believe you will find this book extremely useful. Harrington and Thomas have expertly described how faculty can create and use their syllabi to advance student engagement, learning, and motivation—all of which will lead to greater student success.

Kathleen F. Gabriel
Associate Professor
California State University, Chico

A FUNDAMENTAL CHALLENGE IN HIGHER education is rooted in an assumption that most of us faculty recognize all too well: If one has content knowledge, then the ability to effectively teach that information is a given. Essentially, the assumption purports that if you know it you should be able to teach it. This is believed by many, and it is simply not true.

Many of us realized the invalidity of the assumption when we faced our first classroom full of learners. As a faculty member, for more than 30 years, I have watched the assumption that knowledge comes with the ability to teach play out time and again, frequently in very subtle ways. For example, in acquiring an advanced disciplinary degree, content and research methods are carefully taught throughout the graduate program, while scant attention is given to the growing body of research findings that addresses how to teach any of that content to undergraduate students. How does it make sense that it takes more credentials to teach a 1st-grade class than it does an undergraduate college course?

The good news is that a shift toward recognizing the need to develop instructional skills and continuing to work at being an effective teacher is occurring more and more frequently. Graduate teaching seminars, workshops on teaching strategies specifically designed for graduate students, and better designed graduate teaching assistantships are increasingly prevalent. Centers for teaching and learning continue to be founded and developed to support faculty of all ranks and across all disciplines. Unfortunately, there continues to be insufficient funding and resources to help faculty to establish, maintain, and develop strategies to enhance teaching effectiveness throughout their career as a faculty member.

The Excellent Teacher series is designed to help address instructional resource issues for faculty members throughout higher education. The topics and content in this series are based on over 20 years of my experience as a faculty developer assisting faculty members with enhancing student learning through better teaching strategies. Often, when working with faculty groups, I have asked the question, "What do you find most difficult or challenging in creating effective learning environments for your students?" I have now collected and read literally thousands of responses to this question from faculty throughout the United States and abroad. The responses, along with three decades of experience teaching in a variety of educational settings, have given me a solid understanding of what faculty struggle with, and serve as the foundation for this series. For many titles, I have selected authors or coauthors who are recognized experts in the topic area and share my vision of what faculty are looking for to become better educators.

Our collective objective is to provide you with a strong introductory foundation to each topic in the series. We have written these books with the following specific goals in mind: (a) to maintain accessible language for faculty in all disciplines and with varying levels of teaching experience, (b) to provide you with evidence-based suggestions and strategies, and (c) to provide sufficient background and prompts to give you the confidence to experiment in your own courses. For example, the first book in the series, *Dynamic Lecturing* (Harrington & Zakrajsek, 2017), comes at a time when lecturing is being attacked as ineffective. The book argues that lecturing itself is not a bad teaching strategy, and not all lecturing is ineffective. Research shows that lecturing can be extremely effective when used appropriately and also when paired with engaged learning strategies. *Dynamic Lecturing* provides the rationale and examples of both lectures and engaged learning strategies you can easily adopt. This second book in the series, *Designing a Motivational Syllabus*, provides evidence-based strategies to help you to think critically about what to include in your syllabus and how the syllabus can help students be successful in your course. We argue in this book that the syllabus can be a foundation for the design of the course, a way to build and then share your enthusiasm for the content with your students, and a mechanism to help students to see a learning path that builds their motivation and engagement.

The titles in the series are intended to be interrelated, yet each is self-contained. None presupposes reading of prior volumes. What connects them is a common feel and voice. Jump into whichever topic addresses an area you feel has most relevance to your concerns as a teacher or that appeals to your curiosity as you explore effective ways to engage your students and facilitate their learning of your disciplinary concepts and learning. The concepts and strategies are applicable across all disciplines and to all types of courses, from undergraduate to graduate levels, at all types of institution. The authors draw on workshops given with solid success at research extensive universities, comprehensive undergraduate institutions, private colleges, community and technical colleges, highly selective institutions, and those with open access. There are certainly many differences throughout higher education, but it turns out that there are also some striking similarities when it comes to providing good learning opportunities for our students. Those similarities serve as the foundational themes for these volumes.

The Excellent Teacher series is authored by experienced faculty members who have framed issues and then drawn from the extensive body of research conducted by exceptional individuals from throughout higher education. Our hope is that this series offers fresh approaches to teaching and learning by reviewing traditional methods in light of evidence-based strategies to promote practices that best facilitate student learning. Each volume of the series is written to provide early career faculty with specific strategies that can be quickly implemented, midcareer faculty with the opportunity to adapt and expand on what is currently used, and experienced faculty with new perspectives to augment thinking on foundational aspects of teaching and student learning.

Teaching is important beyond imagination, is anything but easy, and provides us glimpses of the best of humanity, which is why I suspect we all engage in this noblest and most challenging of professions. I do sincerely hope you find this series helpful and wish you well in your teaching endeavors.

Best,
Todd Zakrajsek
University of North Carolina at Chapel Hill

1

HISTORY, VALUE, AND PURPOSE OF THE SYLLABUS

THERE ARE MANY REASONS to think very strategically about your course syllabus. Researchers have found that strong course design has been linked to positive outcomes such as increased student satisfaction, retention, and achievement of student learning outcomes in college (Rienties & Toetenel, 2016; Stewart, Houghton, & Rogers, 2012). In addition, student engagement and motivation have long been linked to higher levels of achievement at the college and university level (Walker, Greene, & Mansell, 2006; Waschull, 2005). As Goodman and colleagues (2011) discovered, students who have higher levels of motivation are more likely to exert more effort on tasks, which in turn leads to higher levels of academic achievement. Knowing the important connection between motivation and achievement, faculty constantly try different teaching and learning techniques aimed at increasing student engagement and motivation. One very powerful and often overlooked motivational tool is the course syllabus.

When professors use the syllabus as a vehicle to share their passion for their discipline and their desire for students to be successful, students become much more excited about the course and learning new content and skills. In other words, the positive energy generated by the faculty member about the course can be contagious. For example, professors can communicate why the course content matters and the benefit of learning the knowledge and skills described in the course learning outcomes. Similarly, when professors use the syllabus to clearly map out a learning path for their students and identify meaningful assignments and learning activities designed to help students achieve the course learning outcomes, students can immediately see the value of learning tasks. Students appreciate it when faculty provide details about the learning tasks and their value, perceiving both the course and the professor in a more positive manner when details mapping out the learning path are provided (Harrington & Gabert-Quillen, 2015).

As the syllabus is typically presented on the first day of class, or sometimes even prior to the start of the semester, it is the first opportunity faculty have to set the stage for future student success. As students begin a new semester, they often experience a variety of emotions. For instance, students may be excited about a new, fresh start and look forward to the learning journey. However, students may also be apprehensive and unsure of what this new learning experience will be like for them. A motivational syllabus that maps out the learning path can foster positive emotions and engagement right from the start of the semester. In other words, the syllabus can set the tone for the positive learning experience that will take place throughout the semester.

Developing or revising a syllabus is also an excellent opportunity for faculty to get excited or reenergized about the course. Thinking seriously about the learning possibilities for the semester can be a very engaging experience for faculty. Taking time out prior to the start of the semester to carefully consider what types of learning activities and tasks will best assist students with achieving the course learning outcomes is time well spent. In addition to this being a motivating task for faculty, creating or redesigning a syllabus is also a planning opportunity. Mapping out the learning path for students will save faculty time throughout the course of the semester. When a well-developed plan has been outlined in the syllabus, faculty will be able to devote their time to implementing effective teaching practices and working with students on an individual basis rather than focusing energy on issues related to course design and assignment development. Perhaps the most rewarding part of a redesigned syllabus that motivates and clearly maps out the learning path is that students will be more likely to achieve at high levels. There is nothing more rewarding than watching students grow and excel!

Unfortunately, many faculty see preparing the syllabus as a mundane ritualistic task of itemizing rules, expectations, and due dates that must be followed or completed each semester rather than as an exciting opportunity to map out the path of learning for students. Because faculty members have numerous responsibilities, of which teaching may not even be the primary focus, many faculty approach the task of revising a syllabus as a clerical one, primarily changing the due dates to reflect the current semester. Some faculty may perceive that they do not have much control over the content and design of the syllabus, as there may be departmental or institutional templates that must be used. As a result, faculty may overlook the importance of this document or view the purpose of this document in a very narrow way, primarily focusing on the syllabus as a document that communicates expectations.

In addition, many faculty view the syllabus primarily as an agreement or as a contractual vehicle to communicate policies. When faculty focus on policies, this can result in a syllabus that has a legalese feel to it. In other words, the syllabus becomes a long list of dos and don'ts rather than a document that focuses on course value, goals, and activities (Wasley, 2008). Rubin (1988) referred to those who create syllabi with a long list of rules about topics such as missing class and turning in work late as "scolders." Scolders view the syllabus as a legal document, a contract of sorts that students latch onto so they can follow the rules of the course. Rubin (1988) also discovered, when working on general education requirements at the University of Maryland, another type of syllabi writers: the "listers." The listers are those faculty members who are trapped into an even older meaning of the syllabus, merely listing readings or topics in some order that is apparent only to them, the syllabus writers.

Reconceptualized as a motivational tool, the syllabus can be an extremely useful resource for students and an opportunity for faculty to think critically about the course as a whole. Faculty can use the syllabus to map out the learning path for students and as a mechanism to start building a learning community within the course. When faculty create a new syllabus, or revise an existing syllabus, it is the perfect opportunity to step back and reflect on the purpose of the syllabus and how to make the most of this important resource. In essence, the syllabus can be used as a motivational course design tool, communicating to students the goals of the course and the path students can take to meet with success. When faculty view the syllabus as a potential tool to enhance the learning experience in terms of motivation, communication, accountability, and curriculum mapping, the end product will be one that will best serve students and faculty. In other words, the syllabus needs to be thought of not as a set of rules and expectations but rather as the foundational document that sets the stage for student success and acts as a planning tool for faculty.

HISTORY OF THE SYLLABUS

The purpose and use of the syllabus has evolved over time. In the seventeenth century, a syllabus was basically a table or index in a book. In the eighteenth century, the term *syllabus* entered the academic realm and became a list of subjects or lectures to be covered in a course (Snyder, 2010). At the turn of the twentieth century, the syllabus became more comprehensive and longer in nature, in part due to the proliferation of photocopying machines in the 1960s that made them easier to reproduce (Snyder, 2010).

One of the most significant shifts related to the content and structure of syllabi was seen in the 1980s when teaching theorists touted the syllabus as a powerful teaching tool, adding many of the conventional elements that we see today, such as learning outcomes (Wasley, 2008). Since that time, teaching and learning professionals have been advocating that the syllabus could be much more than a simple overview of the course, arguing that students would benefit from a syllabus that had more extensive information on assignments, expectations, and resources related to the course. Ganon (2016) and Matejka and Kurke (1994), for instance, suggested that in addition to communicating expectations, the syllabus could also be used as a planning tool or cognitive map for the course. Others have argued that the syllabus could also be used to encourage, guide, and support students (Grunert O'Brien, Millis, & Cohen, 2008; Palmer, Wheeler, & Aneece, 2016).

SYLLABUS AS CONTRACT METAPHOR

One of the most commonly held beliefs about the syllabus is that it is a contract between the professor and the student. But a syllabus is not, in fact, an enforceable contract, as several court cases have concluded (e.g., *Collins v. Grier*, 1983; *Gabriel v. Albany College of Pharmacy and Health Sciences–Vermont Campus*, 2012; *Miller v. MacMurray College*, 2011, as cited in Kauffman, 2014). Kauffman (2014) reiterated that a contract is an agreement, but not every agreement is a contract. A contract must have consideration before it is enforceable, and there is nothing a student gives to a faculty member to constitute consideration (Kauffman, 2014). Consideration is the benefit that each party gains from a contract, such as when you pay for an item at a garage sale and the seller gains money. Many in higher education are tempted to say that the student pays for an education and the faculty member gains a salary, but that contract is between the university and the student and the university and the faculty member, not between the faculty member and the student. In addition, if liability is the legal concern, then the only liability on a faculty member would be if his or her "conduct is alleged to be arbitrary or capricious or to constitute bad faith" (*Collins v. Grier*, 1983, as cited in Kauffman,

2014). It follows that the syllabus should set up a classroom environment that is fair and equitable to all students, should have clearly stated policies and procedures, and should be honest and not misleading. The biggest takeaway from this discussion is that the syllabus has been challenged on legal grounds that it acts as a contract, and to date the syllabus has not been found in courts to be a legally enforceable contract between a faculty member and a student.

Some faculty who view the syllabus as a contract ask their students to sign the syllabus, indicating that they have read and agree to the expectations described. Slattery and Carlson (2005) noted that this practice was even highlighted as a best practice in the literature. However, having students sign the syllabus as if it were a contract is no longer being touted as an exemplar practice because of the tone it sets for the class.

Beyond the fact that a syllabus has not been treated as a contract in our legal system, the "syllabus as a contract" metaphor has negative consequences. Wasley (2008) stated, "A syllabus bloated with legalese and a laundry list of dos and don'ts have turned the teacher–student relationship into an adversarial one" (para. 10). In essence, a long list of rules sends the message that you believe your students are going to engage in inappropriate actions, so it is your job to communicate the rules and potential consequences for breaking them. Although rules and policies are important, Singham (as cited in Wasley, 2008) stated that focusing on rules and policies "turns the classroom into a quasi-courtroom, with students and professors on opposing sides" (para. 48). This goes against everything we think the relationship should be between a student and a professor and has the potential to start the course on a negative tone even before the first class meeting.

Communicating expectations in a more positive way results in better outcomes. Littlefield (1999, as cited in Slattery & Carlson, 2005), for example, found that students were more likely to remember information in a warm, student-friendly syllabus compared to a less student-friendly syllabus. Relatedly, Palmer and colleagues (2016) found, "When students read a learning-focused syllabus, they have significantly more positive perceptions of the document itself, the course described by the syllabus, and the instructor associated with the course" (p. 44). The learning-focused syllabi in this study had a positive, inviting tone, especially in the policy and expectation section. One example of positively stated policy information is "Once in class, it is expected that students will be attentive, including taking notes, and that students will show respect to their classmates and the instructor" (Palmer et al., 2016, p. 41). Another example of a positively stated policy can be found in the Appendix, which contains a sample syllabus. The academic integrity policy in the "Important Policy Information" section on page 157 begins by stating, "All students are expected to engage in academically honest work" and then goes on to talk about the importance and benefits of academic integrity. This contrasts with other syllabi that have a more negative approach, focusing on behaviors students need to avoid and the consequences for not doing so. Perry (2014) added, "Using the business model of a contract gets in the way of learning" (para. 3), and we couldn't agree more. The contract metaphor does not serve teaching and learning goals well.

VALUE OF THE SYLLABUS

Learning is a complex process. There are a number of resources available to help students learn and achieve course goals. As the professor and expert in the field, you are the most important resource. On the basis of your subject matter and pedagogical expertise, you design learning experiences for your students that will help them achieve the learning goals of the course. Throughout the semester, you make yourself available to students to answer their questions and provide assistance with tasks as needed. In addition, you also select and create resources that will support students throughout this learning journey. First and foremost, you determine, perhaps in collaboration with faculty colleagues in your department, the learning outcomes or goals for the course. You also determine the types of assignments or assessments that will provide evidence that students have achieved these learning goals. Finally, you determine what resources, such as the textbook or other materials from the vast literature in the field, and learning activities will best assist students with learning the course content and achieving the goals of the course. The course syllabus is your one resource that pulls it all together and clearly communicates the course goals and learning path.

The syllabus is often the first introduction your students will have to you and your class. Many of us send our syllabus to students via e-mail prior to the start of the semester or post the syllabus in our course learning management system or on the website, giving students the opportunity to see the syllabus prior to meeting us in person. In this case, the syllabus can provide students with an introduction to the course. More specifically, the syllabus communicates the purpose of your course, maps out the learning path for your students, and establishes how you see your role as the course instructor. Some students may even make decisions about whether they will take your course based on the syllabus, as the syllabus can provide a good overview of the course and your teaching approach.

In addition to serving as an introduction to the course, the syllabus is a resource that students can use throughout the semester. Smith and Razzouk (1993) found that the majority of students reported using their syllabus regularly, with 57% indicating that they used their syllabus at least once per week. When a syllabus contains detailed information about assignments, it is more likely that students will regularly refer to it. In these cases, students will view the syllabus as an important resource that will help them meet with success. For example, students will often consult the syllabus to know how to prepare for class, stay on track with due dates, and get guidance on major assignments. Thus, the syllabus has tremendous value to students.

The syllabus is also helpful to faculty. A well-designed syllabus helps faculty stay organized and focused on achieving the learning outcomes. Faculty can review the course schedule to determine if the class is on track and whether adjustments to the schedule are needed. When faculty have clearly articulated policy and assignment expectations, it is also likely that they will receive fewer e-mails with questions. As a result, time with students can be spent on tasks more meaningful than simply clarifying assignment expectations. In other words, creating a syllabus that clearly communicates an overview of the course and specifics related to expectations can be useful from a time management perspective. Although it takes more time to develop a comprehensive and useful syllabus, time can be saved later because students will likely have fewer questions about assignments and other course expectations.

In addition to being a valuable tool for students and faculty, the syllabus can be of benefit to administrators and support personnel. Syllabi provide administrators with a snapshot of the various approaches used in different courses and help them better understand what skills are being targeted for development. Knowing the academic expectations, support services such as the library and tutoring can use this information to guide the services provided. For instance, if using the library databases is an academic skill that is expected, librarians can offer workshops on this topic or develop online tutorials. Likewise, if papers or presentations require students to evaluate information, tutors can be trained on how to best assist students with developing this important cognitive skill. Syllabi can also be reviewed or used by others outside of the college. For instance, four-year colleges often review syllabi from community colleges to determine how courses align for transfer purposes.

Another example of syllabi being used by an outside agency is accreditation. Accrediting bodies may want to review syllabi as part of their analysis because syllabi provide a quick window into the teaching and learning practices at the institution (Doolittle & Siudzinski, 2010). Habanek (2005) and others pointed out that accreditors look specifically for evidence of curricular alignment and program integrity in the syllabus, as accreditors can't observe actual teaching.

PURPOSE OF THE SYLLABUS

Professionals in the teaching and learning field have identified a wide array of purposes of the syllabus. We believe that the syllabus is a powerful document than can serve several functions. The following are three purposes that have been identified in the literature:

1. *Communication tool.* Fornaciari and Dean (2014) stated that one of the primary purposes of the syllabus is to communicate. Others such as Ganon (2016) have agreed, focusing on how faculty can use the syllabus to share an overview of the course and their teaching philosophy and expectations of students. Communicating expectations via the syllabus can prevent misunderstandings (Matejka & Kurke, 1994).

2. *Planning tool.* Another primary purpose of the syllabus is to communicate the course learning outcomes or goals and explain how these goals will be reached through various assignments and activities (Grunert O'Brien et al., 2008). Some researchers have even referred to the syllabus as a cognitive map for the course (Ganon, 2016; Matejka & Kurke, 1994).

3. *Motivational and supportive tool.* Palmer and colleagues (2016) argued that creating a learning-focused syllabus can "positively affect student motivation before students even enter the classroom, making meaningful engagement in the course much more likely" (p. 36). Grunert O'Brien and colleagues (2008) also stated that the syllabus can be used to encourage and guide students, providing students with information and resources to assist them with achieving successful outcomes. Parkes and Harris (2002) noted that the syllabus is a resource for learning.

A Communication Tool

Communication is one of the primary purposes of the syllabus. Rubin (1988) stated, "An inadequate syllabus is a symptom of a larger problem—the lack of communication between teachers and students" (para. 8). Effective faculty–student communication can begin with the syllabus. Students look toward the syllabus to gain a better understanding of the course and what will be expected of them as students in the course. The syllabus should communicate the importance of the course and the knowledge and skills that will be learned as a result of participating in the course. Rubin (1988) argued that a good syllabus provides you with answers to questions such as the following: Why take this course? What are the learning goals or outcomes? What is expected of students in the course? In other words, the syllabus is a tool to share the purpose and learning goals of the course with students. Palmer and colleagues (2016) said that the entire focus of the syllabus should be on course goals, learning activities, and resources available to assist students so that they can meet with success.

In the sample syllabus in the Appendix, you'll see several examples of how learning is integrated throughout the syllabus. One example of how to focus on learning is provided in the "What Is This Course All About?" section of the sample syllabus in the Appendix (see page 152). In this section of the sample syllabus, you will see not only an overview of the course but also an emphasis on the learning outcomes and course content areas. The "What Can I Expect to Happen During Class?" section of the sample syllabus, found on page 154, demonstrates how students may be informed about the different learning experiences that will take place throughout the semester and why these approaches will increase learning. On pages 155 and 156 there is also an entire section on "The Best Way to Study/Learn (According to Research!)."

Palmer (2017) argued that the syllabus is an opportunity to be transparent with students by providing them with a clear overview of the course and expectations. Matejka and Kurke (1994) stated that the syllabus is a "transparent statement of the preliminary work you put into a course—it is a manageable, profound, first impression" (p. 115) of your vision for the course. Research has shown that first impressions can be long lasting. For instance, Buchert, Laws, Apperson, and Bregman (2008) found that the impressions that students formed of their professor very early on in the semester, during the first two weeks, were consistent with their evaluations at the end of the semester. In a similar study, Laws, Apperson, Buchert, and Bregman (2010) found that students formed long-lasting impressions of their professors after the very first class where professors discussed course expectations. Using the syllabus as a way to excite students about the course can help them develop a positive impression about the course and professor and increase student engagement. Further emphasizing the motivational role of the syllabus, Ganon (2016) argued that we can use the syllabus to invite students "to become active learners in our courses" (p. 1). This is consistent with Ken Bain's (n.d.) promising syllabus concept, where he focuses on promising students an intellectually rewarding experience.

In addition to sharing course goals and activities, you can also use the syllabus to communicate your teaching philosophy and to help your students understand what teaching approaches, such as discussion or group activities, will be used throughout the semester and why you use them (Ganon, 2016). A teaching philosophy can give students a sense of the learning environment, including how learning activities will be structured. This can give students a clear picture of the learning experience. In the sample syllabus (Appendix), you will find one example of how to include a teaching philosophy statement in the syllabus (see page 153). In this example, a photo of the professor adds a personal touch, and the text in this section communicates the professor's beliefs and a general overview of the teaching approach that will be used.

A syllabus that clearly communicates course information and expectations demonstrates to students that we have made significant investments in planning the course, and students typically appreciate our efforts (Fornaciari & Dean, 2014). Likewise, having a positive tone and including a teaching philosophy can make you more approachable and increase student motivation (Palmer et al., 2016). Thus, students will appreciate and benefit from our efforts to create a more engaging and effective syllabus.

Another analogy is to view the syllabus as preventative medicine. In other words, use the syllabus as a communication tool that can prevent or at least minimize confusion or conflict (Matejka & Kurke, 1994). When you have clearly articulated policies and expectations, it is less likely that students will need to ask you questions, and when they do, you can use the policies as a guide for responding (Wasley, 2008).

A Planning Tool

Another syllabus metaphor that is often used is the syllabus as a cognitive map (Ganon, 2016; Matejka & Kurke, 1994). We believe this is a particularly strong metaphor. Through the syllabus, faculty can share not only the learning outcomes but also the direct connection between the learning tasks and assignments and the identified learning outcomes. An example of how tasks may be tied to outcomes is located in the "Course Outline" section of the sample syllabus in the Appendix (see page 159). In this example, the course outline has learning objectives, and the purpose and learning goal for each lesson is clearly articulated and linked to the overall course learning outcomes. After each learning objective for the day's lesson, you'll see that the course learning outcome is referenced in parentheses. This approach is also used for the assignments listed in the "Grading Information" section on page 164.

To accomplish this linking, faculty can use a backward design approach (Wiggins & McTighe, 2005) to designing their syllabus and course. The backward design approach requires you to design the course with the end in mind. In other words, first focus on the learning outcomes or goals you have identified for the course. Then, determine what types of assignments would provide you with evidence that students successfully achieved the learning outcomes, and finally, focus on the best teaching methods that will help students achieve the outcomes. We'll explore the use of the backward design approach to syllabus construction more deeply in the next chapter.

In addition to communicating the overall plan for the course, the syllabus can provide a detailed road map, outlining the steps that students will need to take to be successful in the course. Habanek (2005) said that laying out the course schedule shows that you have a plan for the course and that you want students to see that plan—that this isn't some aimless adventure. Use the syllabus to map out the learning path in your course.

A Motivational and Supportive Tool

Research has shown that motivation and engagement are powerful predictors of success (Goodman et al., 2011; Walker et al., 2006; Waschull, 2005). Given this knowledge and the concern about retention and graduation rates across the nation, many colleges and universities have addressed the importance of motivation via professional development opportunities, encouraging faculty to incorporate active learning techniques into their classrooms. Although there is no doubt that the classroom is the best place to engage students, the syllabus can also be used for this purpose.

Slattery and Carlson (2005) argued that the syllabus can most definitely be used as a motivational tool. For example, providing students with action-oriented learning goals and information on how to meet these goals with success can inspire and motivate students. Palmer and colleagues' (2016) research on syllabi further supports the motivational role that syllabi can play. Specifically, the results of their study indicated that students who encountered a learning-focused syllabus viewed the course as more interesting and relevant and the professor as more caring and supportive. According to these researchers, "Learning-focused syllabi are characterized by engaging, question-driven course descriptions; long-ranging, multi-faceted learning goals; clear, measurable learning objectives; robust and transparent assessment and activity descriptions; detailed course schedules; a focus on student success; and, an inviting, approachable, and motivating tone" (p. 36). In another study, Ludy and colleagues (2016) also found that the syllabus could function as a motivational tool. In this study, students responded to a survey after reviewing a syllabus that had more of a contractual feel versus one that was designed to be more engaging. The more engaging version used images and visual tools to package the course content into a more visually appealing document. Results indicated that students who reviewed the engaging syllabus were in fact more interested in the course and also viewed the professor more positively. Specifically, students in this study viewed the professor associated with the engaging syllabus as more encouraging, enthusiastic, and approachable as compared to students who viewed a syllabus that had a more contractual feel (Ludy et al., 2016).

There are various ways to increase motivation via the syllabus. The sample syllabus in the Appendix shows how images designed to motivate students might be used on the very first page of the syllabus, in the section titled "Welcome to Educational Psychology!" (see page 151). The image of children can evoke excitement as students think about themselves as future educators. Visual tools such as white space, bold lettering, under-lining, and a border around text may also be used to make the document more user friendly and engaging. Because many professors are e-mailing or posting the syllabus prior to the start of classes, students are often forming their first impressions of the course based on this document rather than on their interactions with their professors. Although, to our knowledge, there isn't any research on the impact of sending a syllabus out to students prior to the start of class, research on first impressions has shown the importance of the first few interactions with a student (Clayson, 2013; Legg & Wilson, 2009). This was also illustrated in an interesting study conducted by Laws and colleagues (2010). In this study, students were randomly assigned to share their impressions of faculty at the end of the first class or at the end of the first week using an assessment instrument. All students then completed this assessment again at the end of the semester. Results indicated that "enduring first impressions are formed by the end of the first day of class" (Laws et al., 2010, p. 88). Students who participated in this study indicated that the course expectations were clearly communicated on the first day of class. Thus, maximizing the use of the syllabus as a motivational tool can foster high levels of engagement and motivation right from the start of the semester.

Research has found that students' attitudes and actions are often connected to their impression of their professor (Myers & Huebner,

2011; Pass & Neu, 2014). In other words, students are more likely to be motivated to learn and to exert higher levels of effort in a class with a professor whom they view positively. Fornaciari and Dean (2014) found that students appreciate the effort that faculty put into creating a syllabus, so this will likely result in a more positive impression. Through the syllabus, professors can convey their passion for the subject matter and enthusiasm for the course (Habanek, 2005). Positive faculty messages can be contagious, with students also getting excited about the course and ultimately engaging in actions that will be more likely to lead to successful outcomes.

Another way to use the syllabus as a motivational tool is to show your belief in your students and their ability to achieve success. We can communicate this message via a combination of challenging assignments, supportive statements, and emphasis on the availability of support. In the sample syllabus in the "Teaching Philosophy" section on page 153 in the Appendix, an example of this type of message is provided. Specifically, the last part of the first paragraph states, "You will be both challenged and supported throughout this learning experience." These high-level beliefs can translate into high levels of academic achievement. In a classic study conducted by Rosenthal and Jacobson (1968), it was found that teachers' expectations of students influenced the actual achievement of students. Students with teachers who believed in them outperformed students with teachers who did not believe in their ability to be successful. Explicitly telling students you believe in them is therefore important.

Another way to use the syllabus as a motivational tool is to include choices in your syllabus. Choice increases student motivation (Wlodkowski & Ginsberg, 1995). Thus, having a syllabus with a menu of assignment options (i.e., paper, presentation, service-learning project) for students to choose from may also be worth considering as long as all of the options are directly aligned to the course learning outcomes.

MOVING FORWARD

Woods, Luke, and Weir (2010) stated, "Curriculum is what is taught and learned in schools," whereas syllabi are a "bid to shape and set the parameters of a curriculum" (p. 362). Therefore, this book is meant to help you shape and set the parameters of your chosen curriculum. What will your students learn? How will they learn? How will they know *that* they have learned and *what* they have learned? In addition, think about how you motivate students about the curriculum. For instance, how can you get students excited about the knowledge and skills they will gain as a result of the class? How will you engage students in the learning process?

It is hoped that as you read through this book and think about designing or redesigning your syllabus, you will be inspired to reflect on the design of your course in general, carefully considering what learning activities and support will lead to desired outcomes, and the design of your syllabus specifically. In "Applying Course Design Principles to the Syllabus" (chapter 2), the conversation on the syllabus is really an opportunity to look at your course as a whole, possibly making changes to the course structure and learning tasks in addition to repackaging course information into a syllabus that clearly maps out the learning path. Using Wiggins and McTighe's (2005) backward design framework, we'll focus first on identifying and sharing the course learning outcomes. Next, we will explore what assignments or assessments will provide you and your students with strong evidence that the learning outcomes were achieved. The syllabus will be built based on the learning outcomes and assessments identified. Finally, we'll discuss the importance of aligning teaching approaches to the outcomes and how students can learn about your teaching approach through the syllabus.

For those of you who want to give your syllabus a fresh new look but do not have the time at the moment to make significant changes to the overall design of the course, you will find chapters 3, 4, and 5 to be most helpful. These chapters will also be helpful for those of you who are "all in" and are using a backward design process to revise your syllabus. In chapter 3, we'll explore the essential components of a syllabus and why these components are so important. We hope to challenge you to think differently about the content within your syllabus. In chapter 4, we'll ask you to ponder several questions about common policy practices. In chapter 5, we will turn our attention to design considerations, addressing issues such as the tone, organization, and length of the syllabus. You'll discover research that illustrates how simple changes to your syllabus can be quite beneficial to your students.

Chapter 6 is focused on evaluating syllabi. In this chapter, you'll find a syllabus checklist and a syllabus rubric. You may even want to start by reading this chapter and engaging in a self-assessment of your syllabus. This chapter can also be very helpful to teaching and learning center staff or administrators who review and evaluate syllabi on their campus.

Chapter 7 is focused on using the syllabus throughout the semester. Given the importance of this document, this chapter shares strategies that you can use at the beginning of the semester to help students learn how to best use this document as a resource. For example, using icebreaker activities designed around the syllabus not only connects students to one another but also helps students better understand the expectations for the course. Going beyond the initial activities, this section calls for professors to engage students with the syllabus throughout the semester. For instance, using a classroom engagement strategy, such as Turn and Talk, to discuss an upcoming assignment is a way to use the syllabus as a resource and to prepare for upcoming tasks.

Finally, we applaud your openness to change. In this day and age, it is far too easy to just update a few dates on the syllabus and print it out or post it in the learning management system. You are endeavoring to significantly improve your approach to teaching, and the syllabus is a great place to start. Your students will undoubtedly be appreciative of these efforts and will benefit from the time and energy you put into this redesign process.

CHAPTER SUMMARY

The syllabus is an incredibly valuable resource on which students rely. In addition to using this document to communicate essential information about the course, you can use the syllabus as a planning tool. Developing or revising the syllabus for your course is a perfect opportunity to focus on course design, mapping out a learning path for your students to meet with success. Finally, the syllabus can also be used to motivate and engage your students even before class begins. Share your passion and excitement for your discipline, inviting students to partake in a rewarding learning journey with you over the course of the semester.

REFERENCES

Bain, K. (n.d.). The promising syllabus. The Center for Teaching Excellence at New York University. Retrieved from http://kenbain.site.aplus.net/promisingsyllabus.pdf

Buchert, S., Laws, E. L., Apperson, J. M., & Bregman, N. J. (2008). First impressions and professor reputation: Influence on student evaluations of instruction. *Social Psychology of Education: An International Journal, 11*(4), 397–408.

Clayson, D. E. (2013). Initial impressions and the student evaluation of teaching. *Journal of Education for Business, 88*, 26–35.

Doolittle, P. E., & Siudzinski, R. A. (2010). Recommended syllabus components: What do higher education faculty include in their syllabi? *Journal on Excellence in College Teaching, 20*(3), 29–61.

Fornaciari, C. J., & Dean, K. L. (2014). The 21st-century syllabus: From pedagogy to andragogy. *Journal of Management Education, 38*(5), 701–723. doi:10.1177/1052562913504763

Ganon, K. (2016). What goes into a syllabus? *The Chronicle of Higher Education, 63*(9), 1–4.

Goodman, S., Jaffer, T., Keresztesi, M., Mamdani, F., Mokgatle, D., Musariri, M., & . . . Schlechter, A. (2011). An investigation of the relationship between students' motivation and academic performance as mediated by effort. *South African Journal of Psychology, 41*(3), 373–385. doi:10.1177/008124631104100311

Grunert O'Brien, J., Millis, B. J., & Cohen, M. W. (2008). *The course syllabus: A learning-centered approach.* San Francisco, CA: Jossey-Bass.

Habanek, D. V. (2005). An examination of the integrity of the syllabus. *College Teaching, 53*(2), 62–64.

Harrington, C., & Gabert-Quillen, C. (2015). Syllabus length and use of images: An empirical investigation of student perceptions. *Scholarship of Teaching and Learning in Psychology, 1*(3), 235–243.

Kauffman, K. D. (2014, March). *Is your syllabus a contract? A comparison of the SoTL literature and "the law."* Paper presented at the SoTL Commons Conference. Retrieved from http://digitalcommons.georgiasouthern.edu/sotlcommons/SoTL/2014/89

Laws, E. L., Apperson, J. M., Buchert, S., & Bregman, N. J. (2010). Student evaluations of instruction: When are enduring first impressions formed? *North American Journal of Psychology, 12*(1), 81–92.

Legg, A. M., & Wilson, J. H. (2009). E-mail from professor enhances student motivation and attitudes. *Teaching of Psychology, 36*(3), 205–211. doi:10.1080/00986280902960034

Ludy, M., Brackenbury, T., Folkins, J. W., Peet, S. H., Langendorfer, S. J., & Beining, K. (2016). Student impressions of syllabus design: Engaging versus contractual syllabus. *International Journal for the Scholarship of Teaching and Learning, 10*(2), 1–23.

Matejka, K., & Kurke, L. B. (1994). Designing a great syllabus. *College Teaching, 42*(3), 115–117.

Myers, S. A., & Huebner, A. D. (2011). The relationship between students' motives to communicate with their instructors and perceived instructor credibility, attractiveness, and homophily. *College Student Journal, 45*(1), 84–91.

Palmer, M. S. (2017, June). *The science of transparency.* Plenary presentation at the Lilly Teaching and Learning Conference, Bethesda, MD.

Palmer, M. S., Wheeler, L. B., & Aneece, I. (2016). The evolving role of syllabi in higher education. *Change, 48*(4), 36–46.

Parkes, J., & Harris, M. B. (2002). The purposes of a syllabus. *College Teaching, 50*(2), 55–61.

Pass, M. W., & Neu, W. A. (2014). Student effort: The influence of relatedness, competence, and autonomy. *Academy of Educational Leadership Journal, 18*(2), 1–11.

Perry, D. (2014, March 7). Syllabus as contract. Retrieved from http://www.thismess.net/2014/03/syllabus-as-contract.html

Rienties, B., & Toetenel, L. (2016). The impact of learning design on student behaviour, satisfaction and performance: A cross-institutional comparison across 151 modules. *Computers in Human Behavior, 60*, 333–341. doi:10.1016/j.chb.2016.02.074

Rosenthal, R., & Jacobson, L. (1968). *Pygmalion in the classroom: Teacher expectation and pupils' intellectual development*. Bethel, CT: Crown House.

Rubin, S. (1988). Professors, students, and the syllabus. *Graduate Teacher Program Handbook*. Board of Regents, University of Colorado. Retrieved from http://www.colorado.edu/ftep/sites/default/files/attached-files/ftep_memo_to_faculty_10.pdf

Slattery, J. M., & Carlson, J. F. (2005). Preparing an effective syllabus: Current best practices. *College Teaching, 53*(4), 159–164.

Smith, M. F., & Razzouk, N. Y. (1993). Improving classroom communication: The case of the course syllabus. *Journal of Education for Business, 68*(4), 215–222.

Snyder, J. A. (2010). *Brief history of the syllabus with examples*. Derek Bok Center for Teaching and Learning, Harvard University. Retrieved from http://isites.harvard.edu/fs/html/icb.topic58495/syllabushistory.html

Stewart, A. C., Houghton, S. M., & Rogers, P. R. (2012). Instructional design, active learning, and student performance: Using a trading room to teach strategy. *Journal of Management Education, 36*(6), 753–776. doi:10.1177/1052562912456295

Walker, C. O., Greene, B. A., & Mansell, R. A. (2006). Identification with academics, intrinsic/extrinsic motivation, and self-efficacy as predictors of cognitive engagement. *Learning and Individual Differences, 16*(1), 1–12. doi:10.1016/j.lindif.2005.06.004

Waschull, S. B. (2005). Predicting success in online psychology courses: Self-discipline and motivation. *Teaching of Psychology, 32*(3), 190–192. doi:10.1207/s15328023top3203_11

Wasley, P. (2008). The syllabus becomes a repository of legalese. *The Chronicle of Higher Education: The Faculty*. Retrieved from http://www.chronicle.com/article/The-Syllabus-Becomes-a/17723/

Wiggins, G., & McTighe, J. (2005). *Understanding by design* (Expanded 2nd ed.). Upper Saddle River, NJ: Pearson.

Wlodkowski, R. J., & Ginsberg, M. B. (1995). *Diversity and motivation: Culturally responsive teaching in college*. New York, NY: Jossey-Bass.

Woods, A., Luke, A., & Weir, K. (2010). Curriculum and syllabus design. In A. Woods, A. Luke, & K. Weir (Eds.), *Curriculum, syllabus design, and equity: A primer and model* (pp. 362–367). New York, NY: Routledge.

2

APPLYING COURSE DESIGN
PRINCIPLES TO THE SYLLABUS

ALTHOUGH MANY FACULTY VIEW the syllabus as a simple document that informs students about the class and what is expected from them, the syllabus can be so much more. Specifically, the syllabus can be regarded as a course design tool that maps out the learning path for students. Clearly showing students how the assignments and activities will help them achieve the course learning goals can increase motivation and achievement. Students are more likely to be engaged and motivated when they see the meaningfulness of tasks. As we create a new syllabus or revise a previously used syllabus, we can use this as an opportunity to think about the big picture of our course, viewing the syllabus as the document that communicates the vision of, and path toward, success.

There are several different design frameworks that can be used when developing a syllabus and course. Although many faculty use a coverage-based or activity-based design, Wiggins and McTighe (2005) proposed that the backward design is best, and research has provided strong support for this claim (Armbruster, Patel, Johnson, & Weiss, 2009; Reynolds & Kearns, 2017; Wang, Su, Cheung, Wong, & Kwong, 2013). For example, Rienties and Toetenel (2016) found that learning design affected student behavior and performance in both blended and online courses. We agree this is the best approach. After a brief review of the coverage-based and activity-based approaches, we will discuss how revisiting your current syllabi or developing new syllabi through a backward design lens can result in a significantly improved syllabus and course.

COVERAGE-BASED DESIGN

Coverage-based design is one of the most common approaches used by faculty. In the coverage-based approach, faculty design their syllabus around the content that must be covered. Faculty who use this approach begin by deciding which topics or content areas need to be taught. In some cases, the list of core topics is determined at the departmental level and may be provided to instructors who are teaching the course. In other cases, faculty may have the flexibility to determine what content they believe is most essential to the course. After making decisions about what content will be covered, faculty determine how much time will be needed for each topic and the best sequence for the content that will be covered. Then, a course outline that ensures that all of the topics will be adequately covered is developed. This approach is evident in many syllabi.

Many faculty, especially those who are new to teaching, who use the coverage-based design approach rely on the textbook to design their course. In essence, the textbook chapters become the framework for the design of the course. As a result, the course outline often mirrors the textbook chapters. In other words, the course becomes centered around the chapters, with the first week usually targeting chapter 1, the second week targeting chapter 2, and so on. This approach has been prevalent for years, and as a result many textbooks have about 15 chapters to match the length of most semesters. This makes it very easy for faculty to use a chapter-per-week approach to course design. Even when faculty change the order or sequence of how the chapters are covered, the textbook content still often shapes the design of the course.

After outlining when the course content will be addressed, faculty using the coverage-based design approach will then shift to assignments and policies, adding these other essential elements to the syllabus. Because content has been the primary focus during the syllabus development process, it is likely that assignments will focus on building content knowledge. For example, students will often be expected to take exams or write papers that demonstrate that they have learned the content areas identified. This often results in a focus on lower level cognitive learning outcomes. Using the revised version of Bloom's taxonomy as a framework (Anderson & Krathwohl, 2001), this means that most, if not all, of the learning tasks would target the lower levels of the pyramid: remembering and understanding. Tasks that require skill development and higher level cognitive processes may therefore not be as common on the coverage-based design syllabus. Wiggins and McTighe (2005) noted that students often find it challenging to see the "why" behind assignments that are focused on lower level cognitive skills. In other words, students who are asked to simply memorize information may not see the purpose of this task. Not being able to easily understand the reason for, and meaning behind, the task can leave students feeling frustrated and confused about the point or purpose of the course activities.

One of the reasons that the coverage-based approach is used is that it is one of the most efficient ways to create a syllabus. It is neither time-consuming nor complicated to create a course outline that matches the textbook or a list of topics that need to be covered. It really is a simple approach that can be completed relatively quickly. However, it does not necessarily result in high levels of learning.

Although course content is obviously important, effective course design is not based on content or textbook chapters. Rather, the course goals should be the most important factor in course design. Textbooks or other materials should be used to as a supportive resource that will help students achieve the course goals identified by faculty. Focusing on course goals instead of course content puts high-level learning at the center of the course design process. This focus on learning is consistent with Barr and Tagg's (1995) call to shift from a teaching focus to a learning focus. In essence, this call asks faculty to focus on what they want students to learn rather than how they will teach. This paradigm shift is of paramount importance. Concentrating on learning and the goals of the course will lead to more successful outcomes for students.

ACTIVITY-BASED DESIGN

Another approach to course design is the activity-based design framework. Faculty who use this framework focus first on teaching methods. Perhaps the faculty member wants to regularly use group work, try out a new technology tool, or use a simulation or activity that is fun and exciting. In this case, the activities become the driving force behind the design process. Rather than focusing on the learning outcomes, content, or assessment, faculty may be tempted to immediately think about which teaching methods they want to use. Wiggins and McTighe (2005) described this approach as being "hands-on without being minds-on" (p. 16) noting that learning is left to chance when this approach is used.

Research has demonstrated that there is a connection between student engagement and learning (Fredricks, Blumenfeld, & Paris, 2004; Freeman et al., 2014). However, engagement itself does not always lead to learning. It is entirely possible for a student to be having fun and be highly engaged in a class activity but walk away without having learned new knowledge or skills. It is easy for us as faculty to get excited about getting students engaged in a fun activity because the high level of energy in the classroom is rewarding. But Wiggins and McTighe (2005) argued that the activity-based approach will not likely lead to students achieving the course learning outcomes. Focusing instead on the course learning outcomes and identifying active learning exercises that will assist students with successfully achieving the course learning outcomes is more likely to lead to higher levels of student success. It is important to strategically plan our class time in a way that first and foremost facilitates learning. Unfortunately, learning is often left to chance when the activity-based approach is being used.

BACKWARD DESIGN

One of the most widely used course design frameworks is Wiggins and McTighe's (2005) backward design. Researchers have found strong support for the backward design approach to course design. For instance, in a large-scale study at seven different colleges and universities, including community colleges and public and private bachelor's- and graduate-degree-granting institutions, Winkelmes and colleagues (2016) found that students had higher levels of confidence and produced higher quality work when the purpose of assignments was shared. In other words, linking assignments and course goals was valuable. This was true for all students, but especially true for students who were first-generation college students and for students who came from a multiracial background. Further evidence for backward design comes from Levine and colleagues (2008), who found that significant improvements in learning, especially in the areas of foundational knowledge, application, human dimension, and learning how to learn, were found when Fink's taxonomy was used to design courses. Additional evidence for this approach was reported by Fink (2007), who found that faculty using this taxonomy saw higher levels of student learning and improved student morale. Fink's (2013) taxonomy of significant learning and integrated approach to course design focuses on what it is that we want students to learn. Fink proposed six different kinds of learning, some which are cognitive in nature (foundational knowledge, application, and integration) and some which are more affective in nature (learning how to learn, caring, and human dimension). In this taxonomy all these different types of learning are of equal importance and relate to one another.

Creating learning goals for each lecture, aligning assessments and learning goals, and reorganizing the content into broader themes have been found to be connected to significant improvements in self-reported student engagement and increased academic performance (Armbruster et al., 2009). Wang and colleagues' (2013) research lends further support for the value of the backward design approach. Specifically, they found that students in courses where instructors have aligned learning outcomes and assessments, compared to students in less aligned courses, are more likely to adopt deep learning approaches and less likely to use surface learning approaches in the course. Benefits of using backward design were found for both students and instructors in a study conducted by Reynolds and Kearns (2017). In this study, students had higher levels of engagement, and instructors were better able to manage time and prioritize course content. In addition, faculty received more frequent feedback on student comprehension. As you can see, there is solid research support for the backward design approach to course design.

How do you design a course using backward design? The backward design approach requires you to design or develop a course with the end in mind. In other words, the goals drive the planning process. In academia, there are several different terms to describe goals. Refer to Table 2.1 for an overview of goal terms and descriptions.

TABLE 2.1
Goal Terminology

Goal Term	Description
Program learning outcomes	What graduates of a degree program can demonstrate about what they know, think, or are able to do as a result of completing all of the degree requirements.
Course learning outcomes	What students can demonstrate about what they know, think, or are able to do as a result of completing a course.
Class or *module learning objectives*	What students can demonstrate about what they know, think, or are able to do after a participating in a class lesson or online module.

Wiggins and McTighe (2005) identified three steps to designing a course:

1. *Focus on the goals of the course.* Begin the backward course design process with this important question: What is it that you want your students to know, think, or do after successfully completing your course? These desired results are referred to as *course learning outcomes.* Learning outcomes have a center stage role in the design process. In other words, all aspects of the course such as activities or assessments and teaching methods will be selected based on the learning outcomes identified.

2. *Determine what evidence would demonstrate that students have successfully achieved the identified course-level learning outcomes.* This step involves thinking about what types of academic products such as exams, papers, or projects would provide evidence of success for each of the learning outcomes identified for the course. It is important that every learning outcome is assessed. It should be noted that assessments may relate to more than one learning outcome. Therefore, you may be able to use one assessment tool to assess more than one learning outcome. The key issue is that you have determined how you will know if students have achieved each of the course learning outcomes and that this is determined before you begin to think about teaching methods.

3. *Decide which teaching methods and learning activities will best help students achieve the learning outcomes and perform well on the assessments you identified.* Consider which teaching methods or approaches to use in and out of the classroom to help students successfully achieve the goals of the courses. Ask yourself questions such as "When will a lecture or a group activity best help students achieve the learning outcomes?" and "Would the flipped learning or a more traditional approach work best in this situation?" The flipped learning approach is when students watch recorded lectures for homework and then engage in active learning exercises and practice opportunities during class (Bergmann & Sams, 2012).

When you use the backward design process as you develop or revise syllabi, you will be creating a valuable resource for your students. A syllabus developed using the backward design framework will provide students with a clear message about the importance of the course and a road map for being successful, serving students well throughout the semester. Using the backward design process may also help you be more intentional as you create learning pathways for your students. Thinking carefully about the course goals, the evidence for these goals, and the best teaching approaches that will assist students with achieving these goals will help you design your course in a way that will increase student learning. Although many faculty see course design as a process separate from the syllabus, we argue that the syllabus is a snapshot of how your course is designed, and thus course design and syllabus construction go hand in hand. The syllabus is a great vehicle to communicate answers to the big questions such as "Why do I need this course?" and "What will I learn as a result of taking this course?"

Creating a syllabus or even revising a current syllabus may be a time-consuming process. This is especially true the first time you decide to use the backward design framework to guide the syllabus construction process. However, there is no doubt that you will find it to be a rewarding journey. The result will be worth it! By spending time planning out the course, you will find the actual course delivery will become less time-consuming and labor intensive. In other words, spending time on the front end during the design stage will save you time in the long run. This will make it easier for you to balance all of the many tasks you need to complete during the semester. As a result of engaging in the backward design process, the end product will be a strong course guide that maps out a learning path for your students. You will also find backward design thinking to become easier and faster the more you use this approach.

Your students will find the syllabus created using the backward design process to be an incredibly helpful resource that highlights the purpose and goals of the course and explicitly links the course activities and assignments to these goals. Knowing the "why" behind the required activities can increase student engagement, motivation, effort, and ultimately achievement. Schmidt-Wilk (2011) noted that knowing the vision for the course can be inspiring, engaging students right from the start of the semester. Students will most certainly appreciate the work you put into the process of developing a backward-design-based syllabus.

Expanding on the work of Wiggins and McTighe (2005), the following sections map out five steps for faculty to follow in order to redesign their syllabus using a backward design approach.

Step 1: Linking Course and Program Outcomes

Prior to designing your syllabus, step back and reflect on how this particular course fits into program learning outcomes. Program learning outcomes define what graduates of a degree program should know, think, or be able to do as a result of completing the requirements. Courses are selected as part of a curriculum if the course-level goals support the overarching program goals or learning outcomes. Thus, programs and related curricula are typically developed using the backward design framework.

It is important for us to remember that courses are not stand-alone experiences—rather, each course is an important step along the way toward achieving program goals. Courses can introduce skills and knowledge, enhance skills and strengthen knowledge, or foster deeper levels of understanding. One course alone is not expected to be enough to accomplish the identified program learning outcomes, but when partnered with the other required courses in the curriculum, achievement of program learning outcomes can be expected.

Keeping the connection between course and program learning outcomes in mind can help us plan our courses more effectively. Prior to creating your syllabus, begin by asking yourself the following questions:

- Why is this course important?
- How does this course fit into various curricula?
- What will students gain as a result of taking this course?
- How will this course help students achieve the program learning outcomes or build the knowledge and skills relevant to their career path?
- How will this course help students achieve their career goals?

Most syllabi don't tell this story. Sharing how the course fits into the overall program or degree structure is not typically addressed in the syllabus. On the contrary, syllabi typically give an overview of the course without providing the context of how this course fits into the big picture, often never mentioning or highlighting that this course is one step along students' pathway to success. Some syllabi might include information on a general education category such as whether the course will fulfill a social science or humanities elective, but that is typically the extent to which information about the context of the course is communicated. As faculty, we can look at the overall program learning outcomes and easily determine how the course we are teaching can support these overall goals. What is easy for us to see is unlikely to be what our students will see, so articulating how this course connects to program learning outcomes is therefore important. Linking the course to the overall program can immediately add relevance and meaning to the course.

There are different approaches that can be used to communicate the link between the course and the overall program or institutional goals. You can refer to the "Learning Outcomes" section in the sample syllabus (see the Appendix, page 152) to see one example of how to communicate the relationship between a specific course and the overall program. Another approach would be to use a visual tool such as SmartArt, graphs, or tables in the syllabus. This can make it easy for students to see the connections (e.g., see Figure 2.1).

Figure 2.1. Visual approach to sharing connections to program learning outcomes.

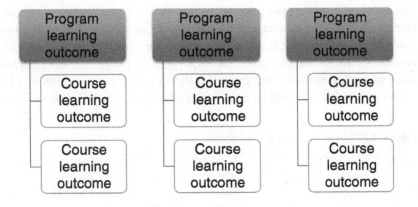

Step 2: Course-Level Learning Outcomes

Once you have provided students with context for the course, it is time to dive into the specifics of the course itself. Woods, Luke, and Weir (2010) emphasized the importance of articulating the outcomes expected of students after they participate in the course. Determining learning outcomes for the course and bringing attention to these outcomes on your syllabus is essential. Unfortunately, students often don't know or are unable to easily recall the course learning outcomes or objectives. This was illustrated in a study conducted by Smith and Razzouk (1993), where almost 30% of the students in the study were not able to recall even 1 of the course learning outcomes, and less than 3% were able to recall more than 2 learning outcomes. Thus, students are taking courses without fully knowing why these courses matter. We can use strategies within the syllabus to draw attention to this important information.

By drawing attention to this section, we can increase the likelihood that students will focus on the purpose and goals of the course. In the sample syllabus, you'll see that a graphic that says "Important" precedes the "Learning Outcomes" section (see page 152 in the Appendix). This is one simple way to help ensure that students attend to this important information.

In some cases, the learning outcomes for courses are developed collaboratively by faculty within a department. This ensures that all students taking different sections of the same course are all focused on the same learning goals. If this is the case for the course you are teaching, you don't need to develop the learning outcomes. However, you will still need to think about how to best communicate these outcomes on the syllabus, as they provide students with extremely important information about the course.

If you are teaching a course that does not already have department-approved learning outcomes, you will want to develop learning outcomes that accurately capture the purpose and goals of the course. Learning outcomes need to communicate the course goals in measurable terms. For guidance in developing learning outcomes, we can turn to Bloom's taxonomy of educational objectives (Bloom, 1956). Although it is still referred to as Bloom's taxonomy, the most significant revision was completed by Anderson and Krathwohl in 2001 (see Figure 2.2). During this revision,

Figure 2.2. Bloom's revised taxonomy.

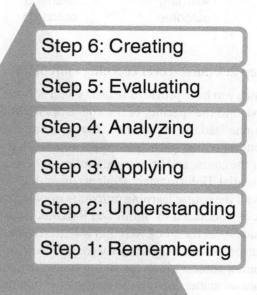

Note. Adapted from *Taxonomy for Learning, Teaching, and Assessing: A Revision of Bloom's Taxonomy of Educational Objectives*, by L. Anderson and D. A. Krathwohl, 2001, New York, NY: Longman.

there were two primary changes. The first change is that nouns were changed to verbs to highlight the active nature of learning. For example, *knowledge* was changed to *remembering*. The second change was to the two highest levels of the pyramid, switching the order of the top two tiers and replacing *synthesize* with *creating*, which is now viewed as the most complex cognitive task (Krathwohl & Anderson, 2010). Educators often use Bloom's taxonomy as a guide when they are developing curriculum and designing courses (Betts, 2008).

As you are considering the nature of your learning outcomes, it is important to think about what level of cognitive engagement you are seeking. Some have argued that there is not enough focus on the higher level cognitive skills in higher education (Roksa & Arum, 2011) and instead the focus has been on lower level cognitive skills such as remembering or recalling facts. Using Bloom's taxonomy can help you carefully consider how much of your course should focus on lower level versus higher level cognitive tasks and can also help ensure that all skill levels are being developed throughout degree programs.

It is important to note that all levels are important and that the goal of using Bloom's taxonomy is to reflect on what it is that we are truly trying to accomplish in each course. The balance between lower level and higher level cognitive tasks can vary depending on the nature of the course and where it falls in the sequencing of the curriculum. For example, an introductory course would likely have a stronger focus on building foundational knowledge, and although it will likely also include higher level cognitive activities to some extent, higher level cognitive tasks may not be a primary focus. The opposite might be true in a graduate or upper division undergraduate course, with a minimal focus on building foundational knowledge and a much larger focus on skills such as analyzing and evaluating. As you can see, Bloom's taxonomy is particularly helpful at assisting faculty with determining and articulating what level of understanding and knowledge they are seeking (Betts, 2008).

An important characteristic of effective learning outcomes is that they are stated in measurable terms (Anderson & Krathwohl, 2001). Learning outcomes should be stated in such a way that it would be easy for an outside observer to know whether the learning outcome was achieved. In the past, we used to say that students would "learn about..." or students would "understand...," but this type of statement does not provide details about the exact knowledge or skills that students would gain as a result of taking the course. Without specific, measurable outcomes, it will be difficult, if not impossible, for students and faculty to know whether the course goals were achieved. Specificity is one of the most important characteristics of goals (Locke & Latham, 2002). Shifting to more measurable terminology is a great way for us to focus on our goals and what we expect from students. In other words, as a result of taking our course, what new knowledge or skills will students walk away with?

Effective learning outcomes often start with the following stem: "At the end of this course, students will be able to . . . ." However, we argue that because the syllabus is a document that is specially designed for students, it makes more sense to personalize this language. Simply replacing the word *student* with *you* can work well for this purpose. To use this approach, you would start the learning outcome stem with "At the end of this course, you will be able to . . . ." Researchers have found that more personalized, conversational language often increases learning (Mayer, 2009), making it more likely that students will recall the course learning outcomes later. In the "Learning Outcomes" section of the sample syllabus (see the Appendix, page 152), you will see examples of course-level learning outcomes. Following each outcome, you'll see that the level of Bloom's taxonomy has also been identified.

Bloom's taxonomy is not the only approach we can turn to for guidance with establishing our learning outcomes. Fink (2013) developed a taxonomy for creating significant learning experiences. There are two primary differences between Fink's (2013) taxonomy and Bloom's (1956) taxonomy. First, Fink's taxonomy for creating significant learning experiences is not hierarchal in nature. Instead, individuals can approach learning through several factors simultaneously. Bloom's taxonomy is hierarchical in nature, assuming that lower level skills need to be developed before higher level skills can be mastered (Anderson & Krathwohl, 2001). Second, Fink's taxonomy is not focused exclusively on cognitive variables; it also includes affective variables in this integrated model rather than addressing these issues with separate taxonomies as Bloom does.

Fink's taxonomy of significant learning focuses on the integration of many learning factors. The six types of significant learning that Fink (2013) identified in his taxonomy are as follows:

1. *Foundational knowledge* refers to remembering and understanding key information and concepts.
2. *Application* involves learners being able to take information learned and apply it to various problems or situations.
3. *Integration* refers to being able to make connections among or between ideas and life situations.
4. *Human dimension* refers to gaining a better understanding of yourself and others.
5. *Caring* focuses on helping individuals develop passion and interest.

6. *Learning how to learn* focuses on assisting learners with increasing their ability to engage in academic self-regulation and actions that will lead to successful outcomes.

Once course learning outcomes have been identified, it is important to figure out the best way to draw attention to these outcomes in the syllabus. One suggestion is to use student-friendly language. Although some students will be familiar with the term *learning outcomes*, others may not. Using simpler terminology can increase students' understanding. Rather than using *learning outcomes* as the heading for this section, consider writing "What will you be able to do after successfully completing this course?" In addition to using student-friendly language, it is also important to draw attention to this section of the syllabus by using a larger font, different color, or even an image. Putting the learning outcomes on the first or second page of the syllabus is also recommended, as this priority placement also communicates importance. See Figure 2.3 for an example of how the learning outcomes might be presented in the syllabus.

Figure 2.3. Sample learning outcomes for a class in developmental psychology.

What will I be able to do after successfully completing this course?

- Identify and discuss key developmental theories and concepts

- Describe how biological, social, and psychological development processes affect individuals across the lifespan

- Apply developmental concepts to situations occurring in everyday life

- Develop oral, visual, and written summaries of developmental concepts

- Summarize and evaluate research findings relevant to developmental psychology

Step 3: Class-Level Learning Objectives

Once you have identified the course-level learning outcomes, it is important to think about how each class period can be used in a way that helps students successfully achieve these learning outcomes. The best way to do this is to identify two or three learning objectives for each class period, lesson, or module. Learning objectives are goals that are more specific in nature than learning outcomes. In other words, the learning outcomes for the course are typically three to five larger goals. Learning objectives are the mini goals that will help students reach the larger course-level goals or learning outcomes. Identifying two or three learning objectives for each lesson will help students see the purpose behind every class. To see several examples of learning objectives, refer to the "Course Outline" section of the sample syllabus (see the Appendix, pages 159–163).

Interestingly, this practice of identifying learning objectives for each class has a stronger presence in online teaching than it does in face-to-face courses. Many online instructors are required to identify learning objectives for each online module or lesson, so online students will often have the benefit of seeing the goals of each module. This is good practice for all modalities of teaching, so it should also be used in face-to-face courses. Having a clear learning goal for each class period can keep you and your students focused and on track to achieve the course-level learning outcomes.

Writing the learning objectives for each class on the syllabus is a great way to map out the learning path. Some researchers have suggested that phrasing the learning objectives in question format may be more engaging for students. For example, Ken Bain (2004) suggested framing each class around a question that will be answered. The question can be the learning objective rephrased. Let's take a look at an example. Perhaps a psychology course has the following as one of the learning objectives for a class: "By the end of class, students will be able to describe classical conditioning." This could be rephrased into a question such as "Why might you experience sadness when a specific song plays on the radio?" Either way, the key issue is that the goals for each class are clearly communicated.

You'll want to be sure that your class-level objectives will in fact help your students meet the overall course-level outcomes. A good way to check that this is the case is to use a learning outcome matrix. In a learning outcome matrix, the larger course-level goals are listed across the top, and the more specific class-level objectives are listed on the left. In the boxes, you can either place a check mark to indicate a connection or, better yet, use letters to indicate a high (H), medium (M), or low (L) level of connection. Empty boxes indicate there is no connection (e.g., see Table 2.2).

In this example, you can see that most course-level outcomes are being addressed by the class-level learning objectives. However, this is not the case for course learning outcome 3. Although class-level learning objectives 4 and 7 are addressing this outcome to some extent, there is a need for increased focus for this goal at the class level. It would therefore be important to add an additional class-level learning objective that more highly connects to this learning outcome. Otherwise, students may not achieve this course-level learning outcome.

TABLE 2.2
Example Learning Outcome Matrix

	Course Learning Outcome 1	Course Learning Outcome 2	Course Learning Outcome 3	Course Learning Outcome 4
Class Learning Objective 1	H	H		
Class Learning Objective 2		L	L	H
Class Learning Objective 3	M	M		
Class Learning Objective 4			L	M
Class Learning Objective 5	L	L		H
Class Learning Objective 6	H	M		M
Class Learning Objective 7		L	M	

Note. H = high level of connection, M = medium level of connection, L = low level of connection. Empty boxes indicate there is no connection.

Step 4: Where's the Evidence? Assignment and Assessments

After you've identified clear learning goals for the course, the next step in the backward design process is to determine summative assessments that will provide evidence that students have successfully achieved the course learning outcomes. Summative assessments are opportunities for students to provide evidence of learning (Wininger, 2005). A final exam and a research project are common examples of summative assessments; however, there are many other types. For example, a group project with a presentation, the development of a website, a portfolio, or a reflection paper are other types of summative assessments. Betts (2008) noted that quizzes are one of the best ways to assess learning outcomes that tap into the lower and medium levels of Bloom's taxonomy and that portfolios and individual and group projects are better suited for goals that tap into the highest levels of Bloom's taxonomy.

It is also important to note that one assessment or assignment may show evidence of more than one learning outcome, so it's not necessary to have a different assessment or assignment for each learning outcome. For example, perhaps you have the following two learning outcomes:

1. Students will be able to summarize the key components of a marketing plan.
2. Students will be able to apply marketing principles to real-world examples.

I'm sure you can imagine several possible assessments or assignments that would demonstrate the achievement of these learning outcomes. A final exam with open-ended questions is one possibility. Because the goal is for students to *summarize* key components, a multiple-choice test would not work well. If, however, the learning outcome was to *recognize* the key components of a marketing plan, then a multiple-choice quiz or test would be appropriate. Another assessment could be a marketing project that requires students to both summarize the key components of a marketing plan and apply marketing principles to an actual business situation. As you can see, each of the example assignments just described provides evidence of both learning outcomes.

Whenever possible, use major assignments that address more than one learning outcome. Having too many major assignments means that students will not have as much time to devote to each one, and this may result in surface-level learning as opposed to deeper learning. Because deep learning requires significant time on task, it is more likely to happen if students are focused on one or two major assignments. When there are just a couple of major assignments that align well to all of the course learning outcomes, students will be able to devote a significant amount of time and effort to these assignments. This will make it more likely that students will achieve the course goals you identified.

Once you have identified the major assignments that align to your course learning outcomes, you can start to map out your course. At this point, you know what you are trying to accomplish and how you will know if the course goals were actually accomplished. The next step is to figure out how to best assist students with performing successfully on these assignments. This typically involves identifying the formative assessment opportunities you can build into your course. Formative assessments are opportunities during the semester that provide students with meaningful feedback about their progress toward successfully completing the major assignments (Wininger, 2005). Research has shown that feedback plays an incredible role in learning (Nicol & Macfarlane-Dick, 2006). In essence, the purpose of formative assessments is to increase student learning by providing helpful feedback. A draft of a paper and a quiz are examples of formative assessments.

The important role of feedback in learning, along with other relatively new findings about how we learn, has prompted many faculty to make significant changes to the structure of their syllabus and course. For example, there was a time when only major assignments such as major exams and research projects were required of students. We are a bit embarrassed to admit that when we first started teaching, our syllabi also reflected this practice. However, using only major assignments or summative assessments is no longer considered best practice. Currently, requiring a combination of formative and summative assessments is considered best practice.

Quizzes, for example, are now frequently required. Research has shown us that testing is not only a way to show what has been learned but also a way to increase learning. Karpicke and Roediger (2007) demonstrated that testing increases later recall of information in a frequently cited study in this area. This phenomenon of increased remembering as a result of being tested frequently has been called the *testing effect* and has shown that testing is a powerful way to learn. Thus, incorporating quizzes into our course design will likely lead to increased student learning. On the basis of feedback related to students' performance on the quizzes, they would be able to make adjustments sooner versus later, if needed, increasing the likelihood that they would be able to perform well on the final exam and demonstrate the achievement of the course learning outcomes.

As you consider what other types of formative assessments to include, ask yourself the following questions about each major assignment:

- What background knowledge will students need to successfully complete this major assignment?
- What skills will students need to successfully complete this major assignment?
- What feedback opportunities can you provide to students to promote accurate self-regulation and successful outcomes?
- What reflection activities can you build into the major assignment to increase learning after the assignment is completed?

The determination of what types of content knowledge and skills are needed for students to successfully complete the summative assessment can guide the design of your course. Let's take a look at the traditional final exam. To perform well on an exam, students will need content knowledge and test-taking strategies. Our teaching practices are probably already focused on helping students develop content knowledge, but we may not be assisting students with developing effective test-taking strategies. By sharing research-based test-taking practices with our students, we would be increasing the likelihood that they will perform well on the test. For example, we could inform students that it is good practice to predict their responses before selecting an answer, read all answer options, eliminate incorrect options, write on their exams, and skip difficult questions when taking a multiple-choice exam (LoSchiavo & Shatz, 2002; McClain, 1983).

Let's look at another example: a group presentation. If the presentation is based on research, students will need information literacy skills, such as finding and evaluating information. Students will also need presentation skills, such as knowing how to develop effective PowerPoint slides or using other media in an effective manner, as well as knowing how to engage the audience and deliver the presentation in a way that increases the likelihood the audience will learn the information presented. Students will also need to know how to effectively work in a group. If you want students to perform well on the group presentation, it may be important to find ways to address these skills during or outside of class.

Consideration of the knowledge and skills needed to achieve the course learning outcomes can help us design our course. If students need these skills to be successful, we may want to incorporate the teaching of these skills into our course or at least point students to outside resources that they can use to develop the skills needed for success in the course. We will therefore want to plan time into the course schedule to help students develop the skills that will contribute to their success. We will also probably want to communicate the rationale for including formative assessments via the syllabus so that students see the value of these tasks and do not misinterpret them as busy work.

Feedback is another essential element of our course and needs to be considered as we engage in the course design or redesign process. Taras (2006) argued that we currently treat undergraduates unfairly because we do not give them enough opportunities to benefit from feedback. In fact, Taras (2006) identified the lack of feedback opportunities as an equity issue, noting that professionals and graduate students are afforded far more opportunities to benefit from feedback than undergraduate students. It is true that most undergraduates are given only one opportunity to write a paper, do a presentation, or take an exam, and although students will typically get feedback on their performance, there is often no opportunity to apply this feedback to improve learning. One of the main reasons for this situation is the large class size that is most frequently seen in undergraduate classrooms, with some courses having hundreds of students in a single section. Despite the challenge of having large numbers of undergraduates each semester, it is essential that we find ways to build feedback opportunities into our course design. At the same time, we need to provide these opportunities in a way that doesn't overly tax our time. The following are a few suggestions of strategies you can consider incorporating into the design of your course.

Require students to submit drafts of final products and provide targeted feedback. Let's use a research paper as an example. You could ask students to submit the references they plan to use to be sure they have found content that matches the goal of the assignment. You could then ask students to submit an outline and a rough draft. Rather than reading and providing feedback on the entire draft, you could inform students that the feedback will be specific in nature. For example, you may provide feedback only on the organizational structure. Targeted feedback is less time-consuming for us as faculty members and also provides students with feedback that is useful but not overwhelming. Sometimes students get discouraged by too much feedback, and this can contribute to more negative views of the course and instructor (Ackerman & Gross, 2010).

Link assignments so feedback on one assignment can be applied to the next assignment. For example, instead of requiring students to do a paper and a group presentation on different topics, consider having these assignments be on the same topic. If you have students complete the paper first and you provide feedback on the paper, this serves two purposes. First, it allows students to use the feedback in the paper as they prepare for the presentation. Second, it also ensures that all group members have something of significance to contribute to the group. Having students complete an activity or assignment before working in a group increases group productivity (Sarfo & Elen, 2011).

Plan to use class time for verbal feedback. When we use class time for feedback, we send a powerful message to students about the important role of feedback in learning. One of the easiest ways to incorporate verbal feedback into class is when students are working together in groups. As the professor, you can walk around to each group and provide feedback on students' progress. Providing face-to-face feedback gives students the opportunity to ask for clarifications if needed, making it more likely that the feedback is understood. Too often students report not understanding written comments (Taylor, 2011). When you provide verbal feedback, you can also be more confident that students are understanding and learning from the feedback.

Incorporate peer feedback opportunities into the course. Using class time for peers to engage in a peer feedback process can be an effective way to increase opportunities for learning from feedback without increasing how much time you need to spend on this process outside of class. However, it is critical that we train students how to give effective feedback. Think about how challenging it can be for us as experts to provide feedback. We can't expect students to know how to do this well without guidance and practice. Many students feel very uncomfortable in this role, because they do not have enough expertise and are unsure of how to provide helpful feedback. Students who receive peer feedback may also be unsure if the feedback is on target. Facey (2011) described a very interesting approach to peer feedback: the peer conveyer belt model. Instead of asking students to provide feedback on an entire paper or other academic product, you would assign students a particular focus for the feedback. To use the peer conveyer belt model, you would divide students into groups, and each group would have a different focus for its feedback. For example, the first group might focus on organization, the second group might focus on whether supporting details are provided for each main idea, and the third group might focus on whether sources were appropriately cited. As the professor, you would briefly train the groups and be sure they fully understand their role and task. Each paper would rotate through the three different groups, being reviewed by a member or two of each group. By the time the paper is returned to the original student, he or she would then have three different types of targeted feedback. In addition to benefiting from the feedback, each student would have also seen several different examples of the assignment, serving as peer models. Although this activity can take up a significant amount of class time, it is worthwhile. Students will benefit from the opportunity to give and receive feedback.

As you can tell, this part of the backward design process is quite complex. Determining the best types of evidence and then working backward to figure out how to help students complete these tasks successfully is not easy. Once you identify the tasks, you then need to figure out how to best communicate the formative and summative assessments via the syllabus. Help students see the value of formative assessments that may not count much toward their final grade by explaining how the purpose of formative assessment is learning.

Step 5: Teaching Approach

The final step in backward design is to determine the best teaching approach that will help students perform well on the assignments and tasks that are aligned with the learning outcomes. Obviously the teaching method or approach can vary from class to class. To determine the best teaching method, begin by looking at the specific learning objectives identified at the class level. Then focus on this question: What teaching approach will best help students achieve the stated objectives for that lesson? If the learning objective is focused on building content knowledge, then the lecture might be the best approach. If, however, the learning objective is focused on skill development, engaging students in group work might be the better teaching approach. A combination of direct instruction and other active learning strategies will likely be needed to achieve the class-level and course-level goals. It is beyond the scope of this book to dive deep into the various teaching methods; refer to Brookfield (2015); Harrington and Zakrajsek (2017); Major, Harris, and Zakrajsek (2016); Nilson (2016); or Silberman and Biech (2015) for a deeper look at teaching approaches.

Although planning ahead of time is essential, good teaching also "requires constant attention and adjustments to ensure that the vision and objectives are achieved" (Schmidt-Wilk, 2011, p. 321). In other words, we need to be somewhat flexible in our teaching approach. Also note that different groups of students will frequently require different types of teaching methods. Using the principles of universal design can help us reach all of our students.

> Universal design for learning (UDL) offers an educational framework for a college instructor that can maximize the design and delivery of course instruction by emphasizing multiple representations of materials, varied means for student expression, content and knowledge, and multiple ways to motivate and engage student learning. (F. G. Smith, 2012, p. 31)

In essence, universal design means you are considering the varied learners in your class as you develop your course. Rather than trying to rigidly map out the teaching approach, you will find that it is best to develop a plan and then modify the plan as needed to help your students achieve at high levels.

Communicating your teaching approach via the syllabus can increase student motivation. One of the best ways to share the teaching approach is to include a brief section within the syllabus on your teaching philosophy. Writing a full teaching philosophy can help you really think about your beliefs about teaching. O'Neal, Meizlish, and Kaplan (n.d.) suggested that you consider big questions such as "How do I know when I've taught successfully?" as well as more targeted questions such as "Why do I teach?" or "What do I believe or value about teaching and student learning?" as you prepare to write your teaching philosophy. As you would imagine, your teaching beliefs will most certainly guide your actions. Refer to Chism (1998), Goodyear and Allchin (1998), Grasha (1996), or Medina and Draugalis (2013) to learn more about writing a teaching philosophy. Although your entire teaching philosophy will not be included in the syllabus, sharing a synopsis of your teaching philosophy in your syllabus can be quite helpful to your students. Consider including a brief section that highlights your beliefs about teaching and gives students a sense of what it will be like to be a student in your class. In the "Teaching Philosophy" and "What Can I Expect to Happen During Class?" sections of the sample syllabus (see the Appendix, pages 153–154), you will see an example of how to give students a brief overview of your teaching beliefs and approach.

Sharing your teaching philosophy and what students can expect to happen during class in your syllabus provides students with a window into your classroom. It communicates the teaching methods that will be used, and students will appreciate having this information. In fact, including a statement about your teaching approach can motivate and engage your students right from the start of the semester. Adding a photo of you and/or your students engaged in learning to this section of the syllabus can also add value, because then it is truly a glimpse into your classroom.

CHAPTER SUMMARY

The backward design approach can be used to help you create or redesign your syllabus. Begin by focusing on the goal, making connections between how the course-level goals fit into the overall program goals. Next, think about the objectives for each class and how these fit together to help students achieve the course-level learning outcomes. Once you have determined the learning outcomes and have made these connections, identify what types of assignments will provide effective evidence that students have successfully achieved the learning outcomes. Finally, consider teaching methods that will best assist students with meeting the stated goals. The final product will be a comprehensive, well-thought-out syllabus that will show students the learning path that will lead to success!

REFERENCES

Ackerman, D. S., & Gross, B. L. (2010). Instructor feedback: How much do students really want? *Journal of Marketing Education*, 32(2), 172–181. doi:10.1177/0273475309360159

Anderson, L., & Krathwohl, D. A. (2001). *Taxonomy for learning, teaching, and assessing: A revision of Bloom's taxonomy of educational objectives.* New York, NY: Longman.

Armbruster, P., Patel, M., Johnson, E., & Weiss, M. (2009). Active learning and student-centered pedagogy improve student attitudes and performance in introductory biology. *CBE Life Sciences Education*, 8(3), 203–213.

Bain, K. (2004). *What the best teachers do.* Cambridge, MA: Harvard University Press.

Barr, R. B., & Tagg, J. (1995). From teaching to learning: A new paradigm for undergraduate education. *Change*, 27(6), 12–25.

Bergmann, J., & Sams, A. (2012). *Flip your classroom: Reach every student, in every class, every time.* Washington, DC: International Society for Technology in Education.

Betts, S. C. (2008). Teaching and assessing basic concepts to advanced application: Using Bloom's taxonomy to inform graduate course design. *Academy of Educational Leadership Journal*, 12(3), 99–106.

Bloom, B. S. (Ed.). (1956). *Taxonomy of educational objectives: The classification of educational goals; Handbook I: Cognitive domain.* White Plains, NY: Longmans, Green.

Brookfield, S. D. (2015). *The skillful teacher: On technique, trust, and responsiveness in the classroom* (3rd ed.). San Francisco, CA: Jossey-Bass.

Chism, N. V. N. (1998). Developing a philosophy of teaching statement. *Essays on Teaching Excellence*, 9(3), 1–2.

Facey, J. (2011, September). "A is for assessment": Strategies for A-level marking to motivate and enable students of all abilities to progress. *Teaching History*, 144, 36–43.

Fink, L. D. (2007). The power of course design to increase student engagement and learning. *Peer Review*, 9(1), 13–17.

Fink, L. D. (2013). *Creating significant learning experiences: An integrated approach to designing college courses* (2nd ed.). San Francisco, CA: Jossey-Bass.

Fredricks, J. A., Blumenfeld, P. C., & Paris, A. H. (2004). School engagement: Potential of the concept, state of the evidence. *Review of Educational Research*, 74(1), 59–109. doi:10.3102/00346543074001059

Freeman, S., Eddy, S. L., McDonough, M., Smith, M. K., Okoroafor, N., Jordt, H., & Wenderoth, M. P. (2014). Active learning increases student performance in science, engineering, and mathematics. *Proceedings of the National Academy of Sciences*, 111(23), 8410–8415. Retrieved from http://www.pnas.org/content/111/23/8410

Goodyear, G. E., & Allchin, D. (1998). Statement of teaching philosophy. *To Improve the Academy*, 17, 103–121.

Grasha, A. F. (1996). *Teaching with style: A practical guide to enhancing learning by understanding teaching and learning styles.* Pittsburgh, PA: Alliance.

Harrington, C., & Zakrajsek, T. (2017). *Dynamic lecturing: Research-based strategies to enhance lecture effectiveness.* Sterling, VA: Stylus.

Karpicke, J. D., & Roediger, H. I. (2007). Repeated retrieval during learning is the key to long-term retention. *Journal of Memory and Language, 57*(2), 151–162. doi:10.1016/j.jml.2006.09.004

Krathwohl, D. R., & Anderson, L. W. (2010). Merlin C. Wittrock and the revision of Bloom's taxonomy. *Educational Psychologist, 45*(1), 64–65.

Levine, L. E., Fallahi, C. R., Nicoll-Senft, J. M., Tessier, J. T., Watson, C. L., & Wood, R. M. (2008). Creating significant learning experiences across disciplines. *College Teaching, 56*(4), 247–254.

Locke, E. A., & Latham, G. P. (2002). Building a practically useful theory of goal setting and task motivation: A 35-year odyssey. *American Psychologist, 57*(9), 705–717. doi:10.1037/0003-066X57.9.705

LoSchiavo, F., & Shatz, M. (2002). Students' reasons for writing on multiple-choice examinations. *Teaching of Psychology, 29*(2), 138–140.

Major, C. H., Harris, M. S., & Zakrajsek, T. (2016). *Teaching for learning: 101 intentionally designed educational activities to put students on the path to success.* New York, NY: Routledge.

Mayer, R. E. (2009). *Multi-media learning* (2nd ed.). New York, NY: Cambridge University Press.

McClain, L. (1983). Behavior during examinations: A comparison of "A," "C," and "F" students. *Teaching of Psychology, 10*(2), 69–71.

Medina, M. S., & Draugalis, J. R. (2013). Writing a teaching philosophy: An evidence-based approach. *American Journal of Health-System Pharmacy, 70*(3), 191–193. doi:10.2146/ajhp120418

Nicol, D. J., & Macfarlane-Dick, D. (2006). Formative assessment and self-regulated learning: A model and seven principles of good feedback practice. *Studies in Higher Education, 31*(2), 199–218.

Nilson, L. B. (2016). *Teaching at its best: A research-based resource for college instructors* (4th ed.). San Francisco, CA: Jossey-Bass.

O'Neal, C., Meizlish, D., & Kaplan, M. (n.d.). *Writing a statement of teaching philosophy for the academic job search* (Occasional Paper No. 23). Center for Research on Learning and Teaching, University of Michigan. Retrieved from http://www.crlt.umich.edu/sites/default/files/resource_files/CRLT_no23.pdf

Reynolds, H. L., & Kearns, K. D. (2017). A planning tool for incorporating backward design, active learning, and authentic assessment in the college classroom. *College Teaching, 65*(1), 17–27.

Rienties, B., & Toetenel, L. (2016). The impact of learning design on student behaviour, satisfaction and performance: A cross-institutional comparison across 151 modules. *Computers in Human Behavior, 60,* 333–341. doi:10.1016/j.chb.2016.02.074

Roksa, J., & Arum, R. (2011). The state of undergraduate learning. *Change: The Magazine of Higher Learning, 43*(2), 35–38.

Sarfo, F., & Elen, J. (2011). Investigating the impact of positive resource interdependence and individual accountability on students' academic performance in cooperative learning. *Electronic Journal of Research in Educational Psychology, 9*(1), 73–93.

Schmidt-Wilk, J. (2011). Course design as a strategic process. *Journal of Management Education, 35*(3), 319–323. doi:10.1177/1052562911407608

Silberman, M., & Biech, E. (2015). *Active training: A handbook of techniques, designs, case examples, and tips* (4th ed.). Hoboken, NJ: Wiley.

Smith, F. G. (2012). Analyzing a college course that adheres to the universal design for learning (UDL) framework. *Journal of the Scholarship of Teaching and Learning, 12*(3), 31–61.

Smith, M. F., & Razzouk, N. Y. (1993). Improving classroom communication: The case of the course syllabus. *Journal of Education for Business, 68*(4), 215–222.

Taras, M. (2006). Do unto others or not: Equity in feedback for undergraduates. *Assessment and Evaluation in Higher Education, 31*(3), 365–377.

Taylor, S. S. (2011). "I really don't know what he meant by that": How well do engineering students understand teachers' comments on their writing? *Technical Communication Quarterly, 20*(2), 139–166. doi:10.1080/10572252.2011.548762

Wang, X., Su, Y., Cheung, S., Wong, E., & Kwong, T. (2013). An exploration of Biggs' constructive alignment in course design and its impact on students' learning approaches. *Assessment and Evaluation in Higher Education, 38*(4), 477–491. doi:10.1080/02602938.2012.658018

Wiggins, G., & McTighe, J. (2005). *Understanding by design* (Expanded 2nd ed.). Upper Saddle River, NJ: Pearson.

Wininger, S. R. (2005). Using your tests to teach: Formative summative assessment. *Teaching of Psychology, 32*(3), 164–166. doi:10.1207/s15328023top3203_7

Winkelmes, M., Bernacki, M., Butler, J., Zochowski, M., Golanics, J., & Weavil, K. H. (2016). A teaching intervention that increases underserved college students' success. *Peer Review, 18*(1–2), 31–36.

Woods, A., Luke, A., & Weir, K. (2010). Curriculum and syllabus design. In A. Woods, A. Luke, & K. Weir (Eds.), *Curriculum, syllabus design, and equity* (pp. 362–367). New York, NY: Routledge.

3

CORE COMPONENTS

STUDENTS ATTEND COLLEGES AND universities with the goal of being successful learners and often rely on the syllabus to serve as a guide to facilitate that success. An effective syllabus provides students with all of the essential information necessary for them to successfully achieve the course goals. In essence, the syllabus maps out the learning path, identifying the tasks that need to be completed, the sequence and timing of course information, the scope and criteria for success, and the expected behaviors of members of the class. This chapter will focus on the course information and assignments aspect of the syllabus; chapter 4 is devoted to course policies and methods for including those policies in the syllabus.

What information do we need to include in a syllabus? Doolittle and Siudzinski (2010) carefully reviewed 15 teaching resources in an effort to identify what syllabus components were most recommended by teaching and learning professionals in higher education. A total of 24 syllabus components were recommended in at least half of the resources reviewed. Doolittle and Siudzinski (2010) then categorized these components into the following 4 major themes:

1. *Course information:* Course name and number; course description or purpose; goals and objectives; location, days, time, and duration; textbook and supplemental reading; content topics; course calendar with due dates
2. *Instructor information:* Instructor name, office hours and location, phone and e-mail address
3. *Grading information:* Grading scale, assignment names, and description

4. *Policy information:* Attendance policy, late and missed work policy, honor code and academic conduct policy (This component is the focus of chapter 4.)

The core elements identified by Doolittle and Siudzinski (2010) represent essential information that needs to be included in our syllabi; however, if we want to create an invitational and motivational syllabus rather than just an informative one, several additional components are in need of consideration. A motivational syllabus provides students with the necessary ingredients to pique interest and encourage the feeling of being part of a community at the start of the semester. As the name implies, this type of syllabus also helps to maintain students' motivation throughout the entire course. Habanek (2005) stated,

> Faculty members should take the contents, intent, and tone of the syllabus seriously. This includes using language that models enthusiasm for the knowledge and skills to be learned, clear outcomes that inform students directly about what they should expect to gain in the course, and complete information about how to be successful in achieving those outcomes. (p. 63)

To create a motivational syllabus, we recommend also including the following components.

5. *A welcome statement and/or a brief overview of your teaching philosophy.* Bain (2004) has argued for years that the syllabus could be used to get students excited about the course and our discipline. A welcoming statement at the start of the syllabus does this by inviting students to our course. It is also a perfect opportunity for us to share a brief biography. Sharing information about our educational and professional backgrounds while also sharing our enthusiasm about our discipline and the course can help students see us as discipline experts who care about learning. Expertise and approachability are qualities that are highly valued by students (Brookfield, 2015). Similarly, sharing our teaching philosophy and helping students understand our approach can really help our students feel more connected to us. The "Teaching Philosophy" section in the sample syllabus (see the Appendix, page 153) contains an example of how to incorporate information about yourself and your teaching philosophy into the syllabus.

6. *Rationale for required assignments.* Students benefit from knowing the "why" behind the learning tasks. When you provide students with the reasons behind the assignments, you can increase their motivation.

As noted by Palmer (2017), sharing the "why" and "how" of learning increases transparency and ultimately student confidence and motivation. In the "Assignment Details and Grading Rubrics" section of the sample syllabus (see page 165 in the Appendix), you will see that the rationale for assignments is shared with students. For example, students taking this educational psychology course are expected to write lesson plans and conduct presentations. The value of these skills as a future educator is described before specifics about the assignments are provided.

7. *Grading rubrics.* Rubrics are tools that can help students better understand your expectations (Reddy & Andrade, 2010). Many professors who use rubrics may opt to provide this information elsewhere, such as within the course learning management system; however, some research has found that students would prefer to receive all of this information at the beginning of the academic term. Specifically, 66% of students indicated that they would prefer to receive a long syllabus with all of the assignment details rather than a shorter syllabus with details following (Harrington & Gabert-Quillen, 2015). Having all the key course resources in one place makes it easier for students to find the information they need to be successful. Students can sometimes become frustrated when they cannot locate details about assignments. Even though the organizational structure we use within the course learning management system makes complete sense to us, students sometimes struggle to locate the documents they need. You'll notice that rubrics follow major assignments in the sample syllabus (see the "Assignment Details and Grading Rubrics" section on page 165 in the Appendix).

8. *Accommodations information.* Although policies in general were recommended by Doolittle and Siudzinski (2010), it is particularly important that we include specific policies related to disability services, including how to access accommodations. In addition to meeting a legal obligation, including a statement about disability services can help students with learning challenges feel more welcomed and become more knowledgeable about how to access accommodations. One way to accomplish this is to include a welcoming statement in addition to providing information about how to access disability services. An example of this approach can be found in the "Important Policy Information" section in the sample syllabus (see the Appendix, page 157).

9. *Resources.* This information can serve as a reminder that support is available, provide students with easy access to campus resources,

and may increase the likelihood of students reaching out for help when needed (Perrine, Lisle, & Tucker, 1995). You'll notice that there is a section titled "Available Help and Support" in the sample syllabus (see the Appendix, page 155). In this table, several of the key campus supports are identified, and information about how to access support is provided.

10. *Tips for success.* Sharing study strategies and other success tips can be helpful to students. Too often, students invest time in study approaches that do not yield high results. By providing students with research-based strategies at the start of the semester, you can increase the likelihood that students will use strategies that are more effective and will therefore lead to higher levels of achievement (Harrington, 2016). For example, McGuire (2015) encouraged students to focus on learning rather than studying, using metacognitive strategies that are more likely to result in long-lasting understanding. In addition to providing students with guidance on how to successfully approach learning tasks, providing tips for success also sends a supportive message, communicating that we want students to be successful. An example of incorporating tips for success into the syllabus can be found in "The Best Way to Study/Learn (According to Research!)" section in the sample syllabus (see page 155 in the Appendix).

Thus, in terms of syllabus content, there are many important elements of a syllabus. Specifically, syllabi should include course information, instructor information, assignment and grading information, policies, and a section on resources and support. See Table 3.1 for a list of specific components to consider when designing a motivational syllabus.

In this chapter, we will focus on the first three components: course information, instructor information, and assignment and grading information. In the next chapter, we will discuss policies and resources that support student success.

COURSE INFORMATION

The most obvious and perhaps important purpose of the syllabus is to share important course information with students. In addition to providing basic information about the course such as the course title, course description, and location and time for classes, this is a good opportunity to share your vision for the course. We can use the syllabus to highlight the purpose and value of the course, emphasize the learning outcomes for the course, make explicit connections between

TABLE 3.1
Essential Components of a Motivational Syllabus

Content Areas	Specific Components
Course information	• Welcome statement • Course name and number • Course description • Purpose, goals, outcomes, and objectives • Location and days, time, and duration • Textbook and supplemental readings • List of topics that will be addressed • Course outline, calendar, and due dates
Instructor information	• Instructor name • Office hours and location • Phone and e-mail address • Brief instructor biography • Brief teaching philosophy statement
Assignment and grading information	• Assignment details • Rationale for assignments, including how assignments link to course learning outcomes • Grading scheme • Weighting of assignments toward final grade • Rubrics
Policies	• Disability policy • Attendance policy • Grading policies, including late and missed work policy • Academic integrity policy • Academic and behavior conduct policy
Resources and supports	• List of campus resources, including contact information for each resource • Tips for being successful in the course

the course learning outcomes and the goals of the students' degree program or their career, and illustrate how the learning objectives for each class connect to the course-level learning outcomes. A motivational syllabus helps students see how the formative assessments and activities lead to the successful achievement of the overall course goals. Providing students with a list of the key content areas that will be addressed and a detailed course outline also helps them see the scope and sequence for the course, allowing them to get a better overall sense of what they will be learning. After reviewing the syllabus, students should walk away with a clear understanding of the course goals and how the assignments and other learning activities fit together to support them with achieving the course-level outcomes.

A course outline or schedule is an important part of the syllabus that can help students see the pace of the course and gets them thinking about how they will need to allocate their time throughout the semester. When using a backward design approach, the course outline comes after identifying the learning outcomes and assignments that provide evidence that students have achieved these learning outcomes. As you develop the schedule, you can begin by focusing on the identified assessments that align to the course learning outcomes and decide when major assignments will be due. Using the backward design process, determine the sequence of content and skill development needed to achieve the course learning goals. The pace should be reasonable both for you and for your students. Look at a calendar and note major campus events and holidays. Think about your own schedule and when you will have other responsibilities. It is a good idea to stagger due dates in different sections of your courses to spread out your grading responsibilities. You'll also want to think about when students will need feedback on early drafts in order to prepare for subsequent assignments. This is an example of when backward design is particularly helpful. Start with when students will need to have the final product finished, then plan backward, determining when the formative assessments related to the final product should be due. Look at the example provided in Table 3.2. In this example, you'll notice that students are taught how to use library databases prior to finding an article and that reading assignments are done prior to class and quizzes after class. This format includes a clear delineation between what is due today, what will be covered, and what will be assigned for the coming class. For the purpose of this example, only a few weeks are included; however, students would find it helpful for this format to be used throughout the semester.

When planning the semester, also consider the campus calendar. What are the important dates that you should know about, such as the last day to drop a course, when midterm grades are due, or when the big sporting events are being held? By paying attention to college-wide events and activities during the planning stage, you will find that it will be less likely that you will need to make adjustments to the calendar later on. Although there may be times that adjustments are needed, students often find changes to the calendar confusing and frustrating.

Garavalia, Hummel, Wiley, and Huitt (1999) found that students and faculty preferred a comprehensive syllabus but also believed that flexibility was important. Flexibility shouldn't change the syllabus in a way that would negatively affect students (e.g., it would be preferable to move a deadline later rather than earlier) or significantly change the way grades are calculated. Flexibility allows for the small changes that naturally occur during the semester, but it is important to note that this flexibility is not the same as an absence of structure (McKeachie & Svinicki, 2005).

TABLE 3.2
Sample Course Schedule Class Topics and Assignments

Class Date	What's Due Today?	Chapter/Topic	Homework/Reading for Next Class
Tuesday 8/19		Introduction to course and overview of resources (i.e., library databases)	Review syllabus. Read chapter 1 and complete reading assignment.
			Locate article on resilience.
Thursday 8/21	Read syllabus and chapter 1 reading assignment.	History, theory, and research strategies	Complete research summary on resilience article.
	Bring in research article on resilience.		
Tuesday 8/26	Research summary on resilience article.	Resilience across the lifespan	Study for chapter 1 quiz.
			Read chapter 2 and complete chapter 2 reading assignment.
Thursday 8/28	Chapter 1 quiz	Biological and environmental factors	Study for chapter 2 quiz.
	Chapter 2 reading assignment		Read chapter 3 and complete chapter 3 reading assignment.
Tuesday 9/2	Chapter 2 quiz	Prenatal development, birth, and the newborn baby	Study for chapter 3 quiz.
	Chapter 3 reading assignment		

INSTRUCTOR INFORMATION

In addition to learning about the course itself, students also want to get to know you, the professor. Learning is a very social activity, and thus relationships can play a very important role in learning. The professor–student relationship really matters. Wilson, Ryan, and Pugh (2010) found that professor–student rapport affected student outcomes. Although rapport is generally established via in-person communications, faculty can use the syllabus to begin building relationships with their students.

Use the syllabus to introduce yourself and inform students about the best way to get in touch with you. By providing contact information such as an e-mail address and phone number, we can make it easier for students to know how to reach out to us when needed. Likewise, sharing our office hours can help students know when we have carved out time specifically to be of assistance to them. Research has shown that students who interact with professors inside and outside of class are more likely to achieve at high levels (Lundberg, 2014).

There are many strategies you can use to increase the likelihood that students will visit you outside of class. Knowing the importance of connections outside of class, some faculty take time during the first week of class to walk students over to their office, as a mini field trip at the end of a class period. This simple act that may take only a few minutes of class time communicates to students your interest in their success and reduces barriers such as confusion about the location of your office. If you plan to use this approach, include "mini field trip to my office" on the syllabus so students know right from the start that you do really want them to connect with you and see you outside of class. You could also offer to meet students at a campus coffee shop, in the hopes of making meeting with you as approachable as possible. Another approach used by faculty is to require students to come to an office hour to receive and review feedback on an assignment or to discuss general progress in the course. This approach is particularly valuable not only because it provides an opportunity for you and your students to connect outside of the classroom but also because feedback provided during a conversation is more likely to be understood and used by students. Research has shown that students often do not understand our written comments, with Taylor (2011) finding that students understood only 55% of comments written by faculty. If feedback is provided verbally during a meeting, students will have the opportunity to ask clarifying questions, and the instructor will have access to nonverbal and verbal feedback that indicates whether students understand the feedback provided. Communicate this approach in the syllabus if you plan to use it. In other words, you could indicate in the course outline that individual professor–student meetings will take place during certain weeks of the course, or you could indicate in the assignment section that feedback is provided during individual meetings in your office. Remember, the goal is to communicate that you want to build relationships with your students and make it easy for them to connect with you outside of class.

In addition to providing basic information about the course, you can include a brief teaching philosophy statement and some biographical information about yourself. As described in the previous chapter, a teaching philosophy statement provides students with a window into your vision of teaching and learning. Students can learn about your beliefs related to teaching and learning and gain a better understanding of the structure and teaching approach that will be used throughout the semester. See O'Neal, Meizlish, and Kaplan (n.d.) for strategies to get started with writing your teaching philosophy. Sharing your teaching philosophy and providing students with a snapshot of your educational and professional experiences can help them see you as an expert in the discipline. This biography is designed not to brag about yourself or intimidate students but rather to give students an idea of your academic interests and how you got to where you are today. As Brookfield (2015) noted, students place high value on expertise and will feel more confident about the learning experience when they perceive the professor to be an authority in the field. In addition, students may wish to discuss your research interest with you or might be interested in discussing career options with you. When we provide a brief biography and our teaching philosophy on the syllabus, we can motivate and engage our students in the learning process. In the sample syllabus, you'll see an example of how to briefly share educational and professional accomplishments (see the "Teaching Philosophy" section in the Appendix, page 153).

ASSIGNMENT AND GRADING INFORMATION

It should come as no surprise that when students were asked to rate the 10 most important syllabus components, the top 3 listed were dates of exams, assignment names and descriptions, and grading (Garavalia et al., 1999). As it's human nature to want to know how you will be assessed before you begin a task, including a list of assignments and a breakdown of the components of graded assessments is useful. Rubrics, which help students see how they will be assessed on each assignment, are also welcome material.

Stevens and Levi (2005) suggested reviewing rubrics with students to be sure that they understand the language and terminology contained within the rubric.

Rather than just receiving a list of assignments, students prefer when we provide details about the assignments within the syllabus (Harrington & Gabert-Quillen, 2015). In fact, researchers have consistently found that students are more likely to view the instructor positively when more detailed information about assignments is provided (Jenkins, Bugeja, & Barber, 2014; Saville, Zinn, Brown, & Marchuk, 2010). Providing assignment details will alleviate students' concerns about what is expected. Instead of simply stating that there will be four exams, provide information about the nature of the exams, such as the following:

> There will be 4 exams that will assess content learned from in- and out-of class learning activities, including the reading assignments. Each of the 4 exams will consist of 50 multiple-choice questions and 5 short-answer questions. There will actually be 7 short-answer questions on the exam, and you will be able to choose which 5 questions you would like to answer. You will be expected to apply content learned to various case scenarios. The final exam is cumulative, meaning the test questions will address content covered throughout the entire semester. Study guides that direct your attention to the most important concepts will be provided.

In addition, guidance or support related to assignments can also be included in the syllabus. Collins (1997) highlighted different types of support we can provide to students about assignments via the syllabus. First is the low-support option:

> Feb 22: Read pages 112–167.

Then there is the high-support option:

> Feb 22: Read pages 112–167.

> This is a particularly complex section on American historiography and theory, followed by application to competing historical representations of the Sand Creek massacre. You may find it most useful to review notes from the lecture on January 30 and pages 77–91 in the textbook prior to doing this new reading. (p. 95)

In this second option, Collins (1997) linked lectures and previous readings to a current reading assignment, thereby reinforcing the study cycle and providing explicit support for his students to be successful in the course. Students often get quite frustrated when they read text but do not walk away with a high level of understanding of the content. This is obviously more likely to occur when the text is particularly challenging. In fact, reading comprehension difficulties was one of the reasons most cited by students for not reading textbooks (Lei, Bartlett, Gorney, & Herschbach, 2010). Research has shown that prior knowledge increases reading comprehension (Recht & Leslie, 1988). Thus, this approach of helping students build their background knowledge prior to reading a challenging section of the text will be useful to them. Sharing these strategies with first-year students is particularly important, as they often need more guidance to meet with success (Talbert, 2017).

Providing a rationale for each assignment or task is also recommended. For example, if you require students to take quizzes, it can be helpful to explain to them why you have them complete quizzes each week. Students are often more motivated to complete assignments and tasks when they understand the value of the tasks. Thus, you might want to consider adding the following explanation for using quizzes to your syllabus:

> Research studies show that one of the most powerful ways to learn is by testing your knowledge (Roediger & Karpicke, 2006). In fact, students who take weekly quizzes outperform students who do not complete weekly quizzes on the final exam (Landrum, 2007). To help you master the course material, you will have the opportunity to take weekly quizzes.

There are several other examples of sharing the rationale for assignments in the sample syllabus. (See the "Assignment Details and Grading Rubrics" section on pages 165–174 in the Appendix.)

Not surprisingly, students want to know how their final grade will be determined. Providing a grading scheme that clearly identifies what final scores are needed for an A, A–, B+, B, B–, and so forth is essential. We will then need to communicate how much each assignment will count toward the final grade. In some cases, your department may determine assignments and their weighting. For example, all faculty may be required to count quizzes as 10%, the final exam as 30%, and so forth. However, in many cases, faculty can determine the weighting of assignments.

Current grading schemes with ranges from 0 to 100 are failure heavy, and the final grade at the end of the semester does not always best capture a student's achievement. Carifio and Carey (2009) argued that grading systems might be fairer and more accurate if the range was from 50 to 100 instead of from 0 to 100, noting that 70% of a typical grading scheme is often associated with a failing grade and that it is next to impossible to recover from a 0 or very low grade on an assignment in this type of grading system. Our task is to be sure that the final grades accurately capture whether students have successfully completed the course learning goals. In other words, the final grade should tell the story of whether course goals were achieved. Averaging scores from a variety of assignments may not accomplish this goal. This averaging approach to final grades, which is frequently used by faculty, means that students' performance at the beginning, middle, and end of the semester counts equally. This will not likely result in a final grade that accurately portrays the level of student learning evident at the completion of the course. When an averaging approach is used, students who performed poorly at the start of the semester, even if they showed tremendous growth throughout the semester, are penalized. In this case, the final grade does not tell the story of how much a student has truly accomplished, because this one grade from early on in the semester pulled down the overall final grade. In fact, some students who receive a poor grade on a high-stakes assignment early on in the semester will know that it may be impossible or nearly impossible to earn the grade they were aiming for and, as a result, may withdraw from the course. In other situations, students may perform well throughout the semester but then because of a personal issue perform poorly on an assignment at the end of the semester. This can be problematic when assessment scores are averaged or if the final assignment is weighted much more heavily than the previous assignments. In many cases, we can reduce the negative impact of these experiences by having a grading system that is flexible in nature.

There are several more effective approaches to grading that will more likely result in an accurate and meaningful final course grade. One approach that doesn't penalize students for not mastering content right at the start of the semester is to use a grading system where assignments at the beginning of the semester count much less than assignments at the end of the semester. For example, if you require 10 writing assignments throughout the semester, the first few writing assignments would not count much, maybe even just 2% of a final grade, but the last few writing assignments would be more heavily weighted, perhaps each counting 10% toward the final grade. This way students can benefit from feedback and engage in learning without being heavily penalized for mistakes made early on in the learning process.

Another approach is to build forgiveness or second-chance policies into the grading policy. For example, some faculty will allow students to drop the lowest exam or assignment grade. Some faculty worry that this approach may result in students not learning as much, as all assignments were carefully designed to align to the course learning outcomes, but if you use this approach with assignments that are similar in nature, this would not be the case. For example, if you give 4 exams, 3 on sections of the course content and 1 cumulative exam on all of the course content, students would be tested on all of the course content even if they didn't take 1 of the exams. Another approach used by many faculty is to allow the cumulative final exam to replace a lower exam grade from earlier in the semester. Similarly, some faculty provide students with the option to redo an assignment or submit an assignment late. Another creative approach described by Hall and colleagues (2001) is second-chance homework. In this approach, students are provided with 2 opportunities to demonstrate what they have learned. After completing a web-based chemistry problem, students are provided with detailed feedback and then given another attempt at a similar problem. It should be noted that in this research study, this second problem was optional but encouraged, as it provided students with the opportunity to increase and demonstrate learning after being provided with feedback. According to Hall and colleagues' research, students who took advantage of the second-chance homework problems demonstrated higher final grades in the course. In addition, students reported spending more time learning the concepts and an increased understanding of the material (Hall et al., 2001). The end result of these approaches will be a final grade that more accurately represents whether learning outcomes have been achieved by the end of the course. One of the biggest advantages associated with this "drop the lowest grade" approach is that it can eliminate outlier grades and increase the likelihood that the final grade accurately reflects students' performance and the achievement of learning outcomes. In addition, student motivation can be positively affected. Grading systems that are more flexible and nimble than the traditional "average all grades across the semester" approach are more likely to accurately capture whether learning outcomes were achieved. Some examples of these grading practices can be found in the sample syllabus. In the "Grading Information" section (see page 164 in the Appendix), you'll see that the first presentation is worth 10% while the second presentation is worth 15% and that the quizzes, midterm exam, and final exam count progressively more toward the final grade. You'll also see in the "Quizzes" section on page 174 that students are informed that they have 3 attempts at each quiz and that the highest grade will count. These approaches enable students to learn from feedback on these learning tasks.

When determining how much to count an assignment toward the final grade, you will want to revisit your learning outcomes. Summative assessments that tap into multiple course learning outcomes might count more than assignments that address a single learning outcome. Similarly, summative assessments should count more than formative assessments. Formative assessments often need to count to increase students' motivation to complete the tasks, but remember the goal of these assessments is to learn, not necessarily to demonstrate knowledge. Many faculty count quizzes or reading assignments, some of the most popular formative assessment techniques, as approximately 10% of the final grade. An example of chapter reading assignments can be found in the "Reading Assignments/Final Exam Review Sheet" section of the sample syllabus (see the Appendix, page 175). We caution against weighting formative assessments too heavily, as it's not appropriate to penalize students for poor performance on tasks that are designed to help them learn. Summative assessments should better tell the story of academic accomplishments at the end of the semester. Remember, the final grade should accurately capture how well students have achieved the course learning outcomes.

What about extra credit? There are two primary reasons that faculty give extra credit opportunities. One reason is to provide students with an opportunity to more deeply engage in course-related content through an additional project or activity. Another reason for extra credit is to give students an additional learning opportunity that can improve their grade in the course if they didn't perform well on a previous task (Lei, 2014). Unfortunately, researchers have found that offering extra credit often doesn't help those who need it most (Harrison, Meister, & LeFevre, 2011). Students who take advantage of extra credit are often the students who already have higher course averages and therefore extra credit may well not serve the purpose of helping students who are struggling in the course (Harrison et al., 2011). Even more interesting was that Harrison and colleagues (2011) looked at several different types of class environments, and students in large lectures were more likely to take advantage of extra credit, most likely because they wanted to stand out from the crowd.

Although not all students take advantage of extra credit opportunities, extra credit does have merit. For example, extra credit can be used as a motivational tool to encourage students to engage in additional learning tasks that require them to dig deeper into course-related content and master it (Kelly, 2013; Norcross, Horrocks, & Stevenson, 1989). Walsh (2009) pointed out that extra credit that has students attend campus events has a positive effect because they engage in the wider college community. When providing extra credit connected to in-class activities, it can encourage class attendance (Wilder, Flood, & Stromsnes, 2001). Sometimes extra credit can provide opportunities for self-testing, which is the case with bonus-point pop quizzes (Thorne, 2000). In the end, whether you decide to offer extra credit in your course depends on your goal. If it is meant to help struggling students, then it has to be carefully crafted and compelling in order to get lower achieving students to complete the task. Lei (2014) cautioned us, though, to be sure that extra credit assignments do not minimize the importance of required assignments and emphasized the need for extra credit opportunities to be aligned to the course learning outcomes. Another reason for caution is that extra credit assignments take time to complete, and this is time that cannot be devoted to other required assignments or learning activities. In other words, extra credit assignments may distract attention and time away from other perhaps more meaningful learning tasks.

Grading systems can be creative. Some faculty choose to use a flexible grading scheme that puts the student and choice at the center of the grading process. Faculty who use this approach provide students with weighting banks or options that allow them to decide, within a given range, how much each assignment will be worth. For example, faculty can inform students that they will need to complete a research project, and this project can count anywhere from 10% to 20% of their final grade. After a discussion, students can then decide if the research project will count as 10%, 15%, or 20% of the final grade. Some faculty also use this approach for the due dates of assignments, giving students a window of time, perhaps a week or so, from which to choose the due date for an assignment. Other professors allow students to choose between different types of assignments. For example, students may opt to write a paper, create a multimedia project, or conduct a presentation to demonstrate in-depth knowledge of the course material. If you decide to incorporate choice, it will be important that you set parameters to ensure that the final grading structure is aligned to the course learning outcomes.

Providing students with grading rubrics will assist them with better understanding the expectations associated with the assignment. As a result, students are more likely to hand in an academic product that meets your expectations. Suskie (2004) described a variety of different types of rubrics:

- *Checklist rubrics* simply list the essential elements of an assignment. Checklist rubrics are the simplest to create and use, but they focus almost exclusively on the presence of content versus the quality of content. They are very useful to remind students about all of the important elements of an assignment but do not provide much guidance on how to create a high-quality product.

- *Holistic rubrics* provide students with an overview of what a product at the A level looks like versus a product at the B, C, D, or F level. Students find the general description of a high-quality product to be useful, but it can be challenging to use this rubric for grading purposes because students may have elements of work at the A, B, and C levels in their academic product. This makes it difficult to assign a grade that is meaningful and accurate.

- *Analytical rubrics* are the most detailed type of rubric. To create an analytical rubric, faculty determine the essential parts or components of the assignment and then describe the characteristics of work at the A, B, C, D, and F levels for each component. As you can imagine, this type of rubric is quite time-consuming to develop, but students find the details provided in this rubric to be quite helpful. The expectations are clearly explained, often with examples. The analytical rubric is also easy to use when grading and provides students with detailed, meaningful feedback about their work. In addition to circling the elements of the rubric that correlate to the student's work, Stevens and Levi (2005) also recommended adding a brief handwritten note with suggestions on how students can improve. Although many faculty do not include rubrics in their syllabus, we believe that including rubrics is helpful to students. You will be creating a comprehensive resource for students that they can regularly refer to throughout the semester. Having all of the essential information about assignments in one place also makes it easier for students to locate the information they need to successfully complete the required academic tasks. Most students prefer this approach of having the rubrics included in the syllabus (Harrington & Gabert-Quillen, 2015).

One last item to consider related to grading information in the syllabus is a grading tracking sheet, which you can see in the Assignment Grade Tracking Form (see Table 3.3). Some faculty provide a worksheet like this for students to fill out to track their course grade. Although many course learning management systems provide this information, it can sometimes be helpful for students to be more actively involved in the process. Using a tracking worksheet allows students to better understand how their final grade is calculated. It can also help students plan for success and can eliminate questions about where they stand. In other words, this technique can empower students to stay up to date on their learning progress.

TABLE 3.3
Assignment Grade Tracking Form

Date	Attended Class?	Date	Attended Class?
1/9		2/25	
1/14		2/27	
1/16		3/11	
1/21		3/13	
1/23		3/18	
1/28		3/20	
1/30		3/27	
2/4		4/1	
2/6		4/3	
2/11		4/8	
2/13		4/10	
2/18		4/15	
2/20		4/17	

Assignment	Value (How much does it count toward the final grade?)	Your Grade
Quiz 1	2%	
Quiz 2	2%	
Quiz 3	2%	
Quiz 4	2%	
Quiz 5	2%	
Reading Assignment 1	2%	
Reading Assignment 2	2%	
Reading Assignment 3	2%	
Reading Assignment 4	2%	
Reading Assignment 5	2%	
Midterm Exam	15%	
Final Exam	25%	
Reflection Paper 1	5%	
Reflection Paper 2	5%	
Research Paper	15%	
Presentation	15%	

CHAPTER SUMMARY

Essential components of a syllabus are motivational when they clearly communicate course expectations and encourage student success. By providing students with detailed information about the course learning outcomes, the assignment and grading information, and the schedule for the course, we are setting the stage for our students to meet with success. As we've discussed, it is important that all of the information about the course is consistent with our overall learning goals. Learning outcomes need to drive the course design process. Students will most certainly appreciate a thoughtful, comprehensive syllabus that maps out a path toward success. Researchers have found that students prefer a syllabus that is comprehensive in nature, providing them with all of the details and information needed to be successful (Harrington & Gabert-Quillen, 2015). Palmer, Wheeler, and Aneece (2016) noted that students appreciate learning-focused syllabi and are subsequently more motivated to participate in the course.

REFERENCES

Bain, K. (2004). *What the best teachers do.* Cambridge, MA: Harvard University Press.

Brookfield, S. D. (2015). *The skillful teacher: On technique, trust, and effectiveness in the classroom* (3rd ed.). San Francisco, CA: Jossey-Bass.

Carifio, J., & Carey, T. (2009). A critical examination of current minimum grading policy recommendations. *The High School Journal, 93*(1), 23–37.

Collins, T. (1997). For openers . . . an inclusive course syllabus. In W. E. Campbell & K. A. Smith (Eds.), *New paradigms for college teaching* (pp. 79–102). Edina, MN: Interaction Books.

Doolittle, P. E., & Siudzinski, R. A. (2010). Recommended syllabus components: What do higher education faculty include in their syllabi? *Journal on Excellence in College Teaching, 20*(3), 29–61.

Garavalia, L. S., Hummel, J. H., Wiley, L. P., & Huitt, W. G. (1999). Constructing the course syllabus: Faculty and student perceptions of important syllabus components. *Journal on Excellence in College Teaching, 10*(1), 5–21.

Habanek, D. V. (2005). An examination of the integrity of the syllabus. *College Teaching, 53*(2), 62–64.

Hall, R. W., Butler, L. G., McGuire, S. Y., McGynn, S. P., Lyon, G. L., Reese, R. L., & Limbach, P. A. (2001). Automated, web-based, second-chance homework. *Journal of Chemical Education, 78*(12), 1704–1708.

Harrington, C. (2016). *Student success in college: Doing what works!* (2nd ed.). Boston, MA: Cengage Learning.

Harrington, C., & Gabert-Quillen, C. (2015). Syllabus length and use of images: An empirical investigation of student perceptions. *Scholarship of Teaching and Learning in Psychology, 1*(3), 235–243.

Harrison, M. A., Meister, D. G., & LeFevre, A. J. (2011). Which students complete extra credit work? *College Student Journal, 550–555.*

Jenkins, J. S., Bugeja, A. D., & Barber, L. K. (2014). More content or more policy? A closer look at syllabus detail, instructor gender, and perception of instructor effectiveness. *College Teaching, 62*(1), 129–135.

Kelly, M. (2013). Extra credit—Dos and don'ts with extra credit. Retrieved from http://712educators.ahout.com/lr/extra credit/145338/1

Landrum, R. (2007). Introductory psychology student performance: Weekly quizzes followed by a cumulative final exam. *Teaching of Psychology, 34*(3), 177–180. doi:10.1080/00986280701498566

Lei, S. A. (2014). Revisiting extra credit assignments: Perspectives of college instructors. *Journal of Instructional Psychology, 40*(1), 14–18.

Lei, S. A., Bartlett, K. A., Gorney, S. E., & Herschbach, T. R. (2010). Resistance to reading compliance among college students: Instructors' perspectives. *College Student Journal, 44*(2), 219–229.

Lundberg, C. A. (2014). Peers and faculty as predictors of learning for community college students. *Community College Review, 42*(2), 79–98. doi:10.1177/0091552113517931

McGuire, S. Y. (2015). *Teach students how to learn: Strategies you can incorporate into any course to improve student metacognition, study skills, and motivation.* Sterling, VA: Stylus.

McKeachie, W. J., & Svinicki, M. (2005). *McKeachie's teaching tips: Strategies, research, and theory for college and university teachers* (12th ed.). Belmont, CA: Wadsworth/Cengage Learning.

Norcross, J. C., Horrocks, L. J., & Stevenson, J. F. (1989). Of barfights and gadflies: Attitudes and practices concerning extra credit in college courses. *Teaching of Psychology, 16*(4), 199–204.

O'Neal, C., Meizlish, D., & Kaplan, M. (n.d.). *Writing a statement of teaching philosophy for the academic job search* (Occasional paper No. 23). Center for Research on Learning and Teaching, University of Michigan. Retrieved from http://www.crlt.umich.edu/sites/default/files/resource_files/CRLT_no23.pdf

Palmer, M. S. (2017, June). *The science of transparency.* Plenary presentation at the Lilly Teaching and Learning Conference, Bethesda, MD.

Palmer, M. S., Wheeler, L. B., & Aneece, I. (2016). The evolving role of syllabi in higher education. *Change, 48*(4), 36–46.

Perrine, R. M., Lisle, J., & Tucker, D. L. (1995). Effects of a syllabus offer of help, student age, and class size on college students' willingness to seek support from faculty. *Journal of Experimental Education, 64*(1), 41–52.

Recht, D. R., & Leslie, L. (1988). Effect of prior knowledge on good and poor readers' memory of text. *Journal of Educational Psychology, 80*(1), 16–20. doi:10.1037/00220663.80.1.16

Reddy, Y. M., & Andrade, H. (2010). A review of rubric use in higher education. *Assessment and Evaluation in Higher Education, 35*(4), 435–448. doi:10.1080/02602930902862859

Roediger, H., & Karpicke, J. D. (2006). Test-enhanced learning: Taking memory tests improves long-term retention. *Psychological Science, 17*(3), 249–255. doi:10.1111/j.1467-9280.2006.01693

Saville, B. K., Zinn, T. E., Brown, A. R., & Marchuk, K. A. (2010). Syllabus detail and students' perceptions of teacher effectiveness. *Teaching of Psychology, 37*(3), 186–189.

Stevens, D. D., & Levi, A. J. (2005). *Introduction to rubrics: An assessment tool to save grading time, convey effective feedback, and promote student learning.* Sterling, VA: Stylus.

Suskie, L. (2004). *Assessing student learning: A common sense guide.* Bolton, MA: Anker.

Talbert, R. (2017). *Flipped learning: A guide for higher education faculty.* Sterling, VA: Stylus.

Taylor, S. S. (2011). "I really don't know what he meant by that": How well do engineering students understand teachers' comments on their writing? *Technical Communication Quarterly, 20*(2), 139–165.doi:10.1080/10572252.2011.548762

Thorne, B. (2000). Extra credit exercise: A painless pop quiz. *Teaching of Psychology, 27*(3), 204–205.

Walsh, M. (2009). Students shaping dialogues at campus events: Ideas for academic engagement. *College Student Journal, 43*(1), 216–220.

Wilder, D., Flood, W., & Stromsnes, W. (2001). The use of random extra credit quizzes to increase student attendance. *Journal of Instructional Psychology, 28*(2), 117–212.

Wilson, J. H., Ryan, R. G., & Pugh, J. L. (2010). Professor–student rapport scale predicts student outcomes. *Teaching of Psychology, 37*, 246–251. doi:10.1080/00986283.2010.510976

4

POLICIES AND RESOURCES

*P*OLICIES AND RESOURCES ARE important components of the syllabus, as they provide students with guidance about what is expected and help students learn about the resources that are available to successfully meet these expectations (Doolittle & Siudzinski, 2010). More specifically, policies can help students understand classroom and institutional norms so that they know the "rules" of the learning environment. By providing students with information about available resources, you increase the likelihood that they will take advantage of these campus supports. In essence, policies and resources provide students with important information about how to be successful in the course.

POLICIES

Policies are used to communicate expectations about classroom behaviors. All too often, however, we include boilerplate worded policies without considering the importance of providing meaningful explanations of those policies. As Collins (1997) explaines,

> To work in higher education is to work in a closed system. Those of us who are insiders to that system go about our business, occasionally surprised by a tacit ground rule we hadn't yet internalized, but for the most part we have been quietly socialized by extended stays in college, then graduate school, to norms we cannot name. (p. 79)

As a first-generation college student himself, Collins (1997) understands why it is so important for faculty to explain policies and the rationales behind them. Sometimes we neglect to provide students with adequate information about our policies, making the faulty assumption that students know the academic rules. For example, Doolittle and Siudzinski (2010) found that of the syllabi they reviewed, only half included an attendance policy; one-third mentioned an honor code policy; one-fourth mentioned a late-work policy, missed-work policy, and disability policy; and only 1 in 10 referenced student support services. Thus, we are often not providing students with important information specifically designed to help them be successful. This lack of information can make it much more challenging for students to be successful. If students are unaware of policies, they may inadvertently violate the rules of the classroom. When we fail to mention disability services policies or support services, students with disabilities may not know how to access the learning accommodations they need and may interpret the absence of this information negatively. Slattery and Carlson (2005) noted that we are doing a disservice to our underserved students when we neglect to include important policy information in our syllabi. Although numerous articles have called for more comprehensive, inclusive, student-centered, and robust syllabi, the call has not been heeded (Doolittle & Siudzinski, 2010).

On the other side of the spectrum is the syllabus that is overly focused on policies. Syllabi written with a heavy emphasis on policies are often composed of an endless list of dos and don'ts about classroom behavior. Frequently, when faculty encounter a problem in their classroom, they add another rule or policy to the syllabus in hopes of preventing this type of situation from arising in the future. Rubin (1988) referred to faculty who use this approach as the "scolders." This approach is problematic for several reasons. First, it sends a negative message to students that you expect that they will engage in inappropriate behaviors if they are not policed on these concepts. Otherwise, why would all these rules be needed? A syllabus filled with rules and policies will not likely engage or motivate students. Rather, a syllabus with endless policies may result in students tuning out and disengaging from the course. It is also not likely that students will use a syllabus that focuses primarily on policies because it may be viewed as an overwhelming, legalese-type document that is not perceived to be valuable. Second, you will never be able to list every possible infraction a student might make. By listing just some of the possible inappropriate behaviors, you are calling attention to these behaviors and perhaps minimizing other behaviors that might be equally problematic. In other words, this approach says that only some inappropriate behaviors matter. Yet another reason that syllabi with a heavy emphasis on policy are not productive is that the focus is on behaviors rather than learning. Learning should take center stage in the syllabus.

Before we shift to looking at specific policies, we want to encourage you to take a step back and reflect on the "why" behind your current policies. It is critical that our policies align with our course goals; policies should support the achievement of the overall goals for the course. Institutional and classroom policies should first and foremost be focused on learning, which is our primary mission. Take a few moments to consider why you have the policies you have. Ask yourself the following questions:

- Where did the policy come from? Did you inherit the policy from someone else? Are there department-, college-, or university-wide policies that you must communicate? Or did you create the policy? Is this policy necessary? Is there research or data available to support the use of this policy?
- If the policy was written long ago, is it still needed? Some policies persist past their relevancy.
- What purpose is the policy supposed to serve? What is the point of the policy?
- How does the policy affect different groups of students? In other words, does this policy promote equity and fairness?
- How does this policy affect the learning process? How does this policy influence the achievement of course learning outcomes?
- Is the policy written in a proactive and positive way?
- What messages do your policies send? How will students interpret your policies?

Some believe that firm policies help students transition to workplace expectations. Kent (2016) cited a survey of employers that identified concerns about the gap in soft skills: 49% of employers found a moderate or large gap between employee skill level and performance level. The skills that were not being met included personal accountability for work, self-motivation, strong work ethic, punctuality, time management, professionalism, and adaptability. Kent (2016) stated, "We do our students a disservice when we provide them with extensions, lax lateness policies, and extra-credit opportunities" and "professors are at the forefront of those who can inculcate these soft skills" (p. 3). Most, if not all, faculty would agree that assisting students with managing their time and engaging in other professional behavior is essential. However, the importance of professionalism needs to be balanced with our overall learning goals. Sometimes faculty's actions communicate that professionalism is more important than learning. Examples of this include a professor who does not allow a student to submit work that is late or who locks the door to prevent students from coming to class late. Although it is likely that these consequences may help students see the importance of timeliness and may even positively affect their time management in the future, the students will miss out on learning opportunities. As a result of not being permitted to enter the class late, students will miss out on the learning activities that took place during class. Because professionalism and learning are both important, the challenge is to determine what type of policy will best support both goals. Whether or not you agree with Kent (2016) and her self-described draconian-seeming rules, she has found that her students "express appreciation for the clarity of my rules, because they always know there they stand" (para. 17). However, there are other approaches that can work just as well or perhaps even better in helping students develop skills related to professionalism. Instead of not permitting students to enter a class late, you can have a policy that communicates the importance of arriving on time for class and provides guidance to students on what to do if they do arrive late on occasion. For example, you could tell students to quietly enter the classroom and avoid walking in front of you to get to their seat.

Policies can promote equity. Treating students fairly and with respect is essential. One of the problems with rigid policies is that we may see a valid reason for granting an exception and then are in the difficult situation of deciding what to do in that situation. Let's take a look at an example. If you have a "no makeup exam" policy on your syllabus, but one of your students was in a car accident and was hospitalized or was just informed that a close family member died, would you stick to your policy? Most of us would probably say that we would likely make an exception. Although one might be hard-pressed to argue against the spirit of this policy, as it promotes good time management and professionalism, consider how this policy might differently affect students from various cultural backgrounds. If this student is from a culture where it is acceptable and sometimes even encouraged to challenge rules, the student will likely approach you and ask to take the exam on a different day. If, however, this student is from a culture where challenging the rules or an authority figure is frowned upon, the student may never reach out to you, believing the rule is the rule. You would therefore be unaware of the situation and would not be able to make an exception and offer a makeup exam. One solution to this dilemma is to create flexible policies. Instead of having a "no makeup exam" policy, what about having a policy that promotes timeliness but builds in flexibility to accommodate for life circumstances that may arise? Consider the following example:

> It is important to stay on track with your assignments and take exams on schedule; not only will this help you feel less stressed, but it is also an important skill you will need in your career. Being able to meet deadlines and juggle many tasks is an important career and life skill. Thus, it is expected that you will complete all assignments and exams according to the schedule. If you have a personal situation that prevents you from doing so, please discuss this with me prior to the due date, if possible, so we can explore options. If it is not possible to discuss this prior to the due date, please reach out as soon as it is possible to do so. While effective time management is an essential skill, I understand that life circumstances can sometimes make this challenging or impossible.

Once we have carefully considered the value of our policies, we will then want to clearly communicate these policies in a positive way. Using more positive language and capturing the overall focus or spirit of the policy is a good approach. Slattery and Carlson (2005) believed that a warm syllabus tone can "anticipate positive student outcomes, rather than merely attempting to prevent problems" (p. 159). Therefore, the overall tone of how policies are written can affect how students achieve and the level of trust and open communication we have with our students. For example, instead of saying "Do not use your phones in class" in your syllabus, consider sending the following more positive and comprehensive message: "All students are expected to engage in behaviors that foster a learning-focused environment and are consistent with the behaviors outlined in the code of student conduct." If you prefer to specifically address cell phones, consider the following: "Creating a learning-focused environment is very important to me. Because research has found that learning is negatively affected when students use their cell phone for nonacademic purposes during class, we will all need to refrain from using cell phones during class (End, Worthman, Mathews, & Wetterau, 2010)."

Do you express to your students why policies are important? For instance, if you have a "no laptops" policy, you could share research that shows that when students engage in multitasking on their laptop during class, it negatively affects their success and the success of their classmates (Sana, Weston, & Cepeda, 2013). You could also emphasize how laptops and cell phones can get in the way of an experiential classroom, where they learn by doing and engaging with each other. When you provide a rationale, you help students understand the need for and importance of the policy.

Hutcheon (2017) cautioned us to consider the impact of our policies on student motivation. In this study, students were randomly assigned to a class with a technology ban that did not allow students to use laptops or other technology tools or to a class permitted to use technology. Results indicated that students in the class with the technology ban had lower levels of motivation and engagement as compared to students in the class where technology was permitted. In essence, Hutcheon (2017) encouraged us to carefully review the reasons and data behind our policies and their potential consequences. In this example related to technology use in the classroom, there are several studies that suggest laptop use in the classroom can negatively affect learning; however, Hutcheon (2017) noted that statistically significant findings are not always clinically significant findings, and the learning environment is so complex that the impact of policies in different environments is likely to vary substantially. As you develop classroom policies, keep in mind the potential positive and negative impacts of the policies you are creating and align these policies with your learning objectives.

Finally, it is essential that our class policies align with departmental or institutional policies. In other words, the policies you develop should not conflict with policies already established at your institution. If policies do conflict, students will be confused about what rule to follow and have a strong position from which to challenge your course policy. For example, if there are department or university policies on attendance, your class-level policy needs to be consistent with these already established policies. If the standardized policies that you are required to include in your syllabus are written in a way that is not consistent with the positive tone you are striving for, find out if you can modify the language. You may be able to make minor edits, such as changing "students" to "you." If you are not permitted to modify the policy language, you may want to consider adding introductory text that emphasizes the messages you want to send prior to the boilerplate policy information you must include.

Learning Accommodations for Students With Disabilities

Most colleges and universities provide some sort of standardized language for the syllabus to indicate that the professor will provide reasonable accommodations for students with disabilities. Thus, it is important to find out if your department, college, or university has already established policy language related to students with disabilities that you will need to include. If your college or university does not require specific policy language, you can reach out to Disability Services for guidance. Wood and Madden (2014) stated, "Students with disabilities, especially those whose

needs may not be met under the minimum legal guidelines for accommodations, can glean a lot from the accommodation statement in the syllabus
about how the instructor approaches disability; this statement reveals the
teacher's ethos as well as her attitude toward issues of access" (para. 1).
Wood and Madden (2014) went on to encourage going beyond the legalis-
tic minimums and crafting statements that give students "adaptable, universal access to our pedagogies and classroom spaces" (para. 1). You can
also take such boilerplate language and make it more accessible, such as
the following:

> I honor your place in this classroom and your ability to learn. To ensure
> that all students with learning challenges have a positive learning envi-
> ronment, the following is the university's disability accomodations
> statement required to appear on each syllabus:
>
> > Please provide me with the accommodations paperwork from the
> > Disability Services Office during the first two weeks of this course.
> > I want to provide you the best learning environment possible. Even
> > if you don't have a documented disability, please know that there
> > are services available to all students at the university that can sup-
> > port your learning, including the International Students Office,
> > Writing Center, Learning Center, and Counseling Center.

Language matters. Language can affect how students respond to you and
your course. For policies that have legal ramifications, such as with disability policies, language is critical. Thus, it is important to seek guidance
as you develop your disability policy. Reach out to your chairperson or
dean to find out if standardized language already exists, and if it doesn't,
consult with the disability services provider on your campus to determine
if the policy language you develop is consistent with disability law and
institutional policies and will increase the likelihood of students accessing learning accommodations if needed. Disability policies and statements
belong in the beginning of the syllabus so that students can easily access
them. Use language that students are more likely to be familiar with, and
avoid terminology that students may not know. For example, Wood and
Madden (2014) cautioned about using the term *universal design* as the title
for this policy, because it can be confusing to students who have never
heard of that term. Instead, identify a title with inclusivity in mind, such
as "Inclusive Learning Statement," "Learning Accommodations," "Accessibility Statement," and so forth. Titling the section "Disability Services" or
"Accommodations" can work well too, because students will be able to find
this section easily. The grander issue is that you stand behind the statement

in your syllabus, you uphold the law, and you believe in making your classroom and your teaching accessible to all students.

Attendance Policies

As with all policies, first determine if your department, college, or university has an institutional attendance policy. If this is the case, you will need to either use the institutional policy language or at least be sure that your class-level policies related to attendance are consistent with the institution. It is important that we don't send mixed messages to our students; this can cause confusion about expectations. In the absence of an institutional policy, you will need to consider the need for an attendance policy at the class level.

To determine the need for an attendance policy, consider this question: "Why is class attendance important?" According to research, class attendance has a significant impact on exam performance. Moreover, "the more frequently a student attends lectures, the greater the benefits obtained from attending" (Chen & Lin, 2010, p. 224). Crede, Roch, and Kieszczynka (2010) found in their meta-analytic review that class attendance was strongly correlated with class and cumulative grades and was an even better predictor of college success than SAT scores, high school GPA, study habits, or study skills. Furthermore, Gump (2013) stated as a conclusion of his research, "Students who wish to succeed academically should attend class, and instructors should likewise encourage class attendance" (p. 1). Given these research findings that illustrate the important role of attendance in achievement, having a policy on attendance may help your students reach their goals.

In contrast, St. Clair (1999) argued against compulsory attendance policies using a motivational construct: "Classroom environments that engage students, emphasize the importance of students' contributions, and have content directly related to knowledge assessed will undoubtedly provide encouragement to students to attend regularly" (pp. 177–178). According to this argument, policy may not be the best way to influence behavior. Instead, using engaging and effective teaching strategies will have more of an impact on whether students attend class. Thus, the question here is "Is an attendance policy necessary?" St. Clair (1999) raised the issue that if tracking attendance is mandated by an external factor, then you have to work within those bounds.

Although all would agree that attendance is connected to successful outcomes, the issue is how to increase student attendance. We could simply encourage students to attend, emphasizing how attendance is linked to student achievement. We could also motivate students to attend class and arrive on time by offering a bonus quiz at the start of class. Bonus quizzes are brief quizzes that provide students with extra credit points on an exam or other assignment. The beauty of this approach is that it rewards students who attend class but does not penalize students who are late or miss a class. The other option is to make attendance mandatory, tying attendance to final grades in some way.

Moore (2005) conducted some interesting research on whether penalties were more effective than rewards in order to influence class attendance. Results indicated that intense penalties did not improve students' attendance rates and detrimentally affected the passing rates of his course (Moore, 2005). This raises an important issue. Grades should reflect a student's progress toward the course learning outcomes, yet sometimes policies can get in the way of a grade accurately capturing a student's achievement. Attendance policies with severe consequences, such as dropping a student's grade based on a few absences, often negatively affect grades in a significant way. The policy was probably established to improve student performance and motivate students to attend class. However, it is important for us to recognize the fact that students may be able to still meet the course learning outcomes even if they missed a few classes. There will, of course, be situations where it is not possible for a student to achieve a learning outcome if he or she is absent from class a few times. For example, in a hands-on learning environment where students are preparing and serving meals in a hospitality course, the student may not be able to earn any credit for this assignment. In this situation, the natural consequence is that the grade will be negatively affected so it may not be necessary to add another negative grade related to attendance. As we develop our policies, we need to keep in mind the purpose and potential consequences of our policies. Do we really want a student who has demonstrated a high level of proficiency on the assessments we used to have a grade that is much lower because he or she missed a few classes? The importance of class attendance varies from discipline to discipline and from course to course, so it is critical that we look at the unique factors and learning outcomes for each course to make a decision.

If you decide to give credit for attendance, there are a variety of approaches you can use. One strategy that is widely used by faculty is to include a participation grade whereby students earn points by participating in discussions and group activities. To earn points for these activities, students need to be in class. But you should consider how you will track participation and what constitutes participation. For instance, many faculty use an index card system where students fill out a card at the beginning of the semester and then as students participate, a mark is made. Faculty can also use the cards to take turns asking for participation. Another way to track participation is to have a piece of cardstock printed for each student with the days of the semester in the left-hand column and a space to write in the right-hand column. Each day you could pose an entering question and exiting question to see how students engaged with that day's content and learning. Technology is of course another option. There are many technology tools, including several in learning management systems, that can assist faculty with keeping track of attendance. For example, attendance and participation could be done electronically through a system like Kahoot! or a clicker system. Another approach is to give quizzes at the start of class that count either toward the final grade or as extra credit points. Padilla-Walker (2006) found that extra credit quizzes increased student motivation and achievement. Of course, it is also possible simply to record attendance, giving credit to students for physically being present in class.

If you decide to grade participation or attendance, you will probably want this to count as only a small portion of the final grade, perhaps 5% to 10% to avoid students earning grades that do not accurately capture how much they learned. Although attending and participating in class is important, much more is needed to demonstrate that real learning took place. Using these strategies can motivate your students to attend.

Late and Missed Work Policies

We would all agree that completing tasks on schedule is important, but there will undoubtedly be situations where students do not submit an assignment on time. Late and missed work policies can communicate the importance of completing tasks in a timely manner and outline the consequences associated with not submitting work according to the course schedule. Unfortunately, late and missed work policies are not always included in course syllabi. In fact, only 20% of the syllabi reviewed in a study by Doolittle and Siudzinski (2010) included late and missed work policies. To determine what type of late and missed work policy to use in class, many faculty begin by asking themselves several questions, such as "If a student does not submit an assignment on time, will I accept it late?" and "If so, is there a penalty, and if so, what is that penalty?" One of the reasons that faculty prefer a "no late work" policy is that it removes the burden associated with determining what situations warrant an extension or exception to the rule. However, life is complex, and a rigid policy may not be the best way to foster learning.

Perhaps the better question is "What late or missed work policies will best support the goals of the course?" This can be challenging when you have two competing goals such as developing professional skills (e.g., effective time management) and learning the knowledge and skills associated with the course content. A "no late work" policy will support the professional goal but not the learning goal, as students will miss out on the learning experience associated with the assignment. When you have competing goals, you will need to consider the importance of each goal. This can help guide your decision-making as you develop grading policies.

There are those faculty who have decided that their syllabi have accumulated too many rigid policies and legalese over the years and have moved to strip it out of their syllabi. Wasley (2008) decided to delete her zero tolerance for late work and said that "the world did not crumble" (p. 6), but the change did create better conversations with students than if she had kept that legalese in her syllabus.

A 0 on a large assignment (with no opportunities to earn even partial credit with a late submission) can have devastating consequences on a student's overall course grade, GPA, financial aid, and level of motivation. Guskey (2004) stated, "If the grade is to represent how well students have learned, mastered established learning standards, or achieved specified learning goals, then the practice of assigning zeros clearly misses the mark" (p. 33), noting that a final grade in a course where a student earned 0 points on an assignment does not accurately reflect the learning that took place. It is difficult, if not impossible, for a student to recover from a 0 grade, especially on high-stakes assignments. For example, consider a course in which a total of 400 points is possible: 3 exams and a term paper, each worth 100 points. If the paper received a 0, then a student with a 90% average on all 3 exams would end up with an average of 67.5% (3 exams at 90 points each and 1 paper at 0 points for a total of 270 out of 400 possible points). Low grades may cause students to become discouraged and perhaps withdraw from the course.

One solution is to avoid stand-alone high-stakes assignments. Instead of just requiring students to submit a final paper, build in formative assignments throughout the semester. In essence, build up to a final assignment in a way that makes it impossible for students to get a zero on the entire project unless the deadline for each step of the project was missed. For instance, a group assignment that spans the semester and has several pieces to it, including a paper, video, poster presentation, and peer review, would make it virtually impossible for students to miss each deadline along the way. In the event that a student does not submit one portion, it would not be a grade killer. In other words, provide students with

many opportunities to demonstrate their knowledge and skills throughout the semester.

Another potential solution to this dilemma is to allow students to submit work late for partial credit. You will, however, need to determine the
level of point reduction for late work. Some faculty who accept late work
offer some serious consequences, such as only offering up to half credit for
late work or a reduction in a letter grade for every day it is late. Although
policies such as these on the surface communicate some flexibility and
a willingness to work with students, the reality is that these policies can
still have a significant negative impact on the final grade and on student
motivation. Half credit on an assignment is much better than a zero, but
it can still be quite discouraging and difficult to recover from. Many students may not view half credit as being enough of an incentive to submit
the work late. Likewise, if a student did not submit an assignment on time,
having only an extra day or two might not be enough if he or she was
seriously ill or coping with a death of a loved one. Thus, you may want to
consider more flexible late work policies. Some faculty have a onetime pass
at the end of the semester, allowing students to submit one assignment that
was not previously completed. This onetime pass can be without any penalty or may come with a minor reduction in points on the assignment. You
may want to think about this opportunity in a broader sense, allowing students to redo one assignment even if it was submitted. Knowing that these
assignments will be submitted during this one-week time period allows
you to plan ahead with your schedule. Consider the following example:

> All students will have the opportunity to submit one assignment that
> was missed or redo an assignment during the last week of the semester.
> There will be no penalty for lateness.

Another way to approach a late work policy is to have different rules for
different types of assignments. You might want to have a no late work
policy for very low-stakes assignments such as quizzes or reading assignments but have a more flexible policy for high-stakes assignments. For
an example of how quizzes and reading assignments can be used as low-
stakes assignments, see the "Quizzes" and "Reading Assignments/Final
Exam Review Sheet" sections of the sample syllabus on pages 174 and 175
in the Appendix. The rationale for different rules for different assignments
is that a zero on a low-stakes assignment will not affect the final grade
much, if at all, but a zero on a high-stakes assignment could have a huge
impact on the final grade for the course. If you decide to use this approach,
this means that you won't necessarily always accept late work on major

assignments but rather that this is a possibility. This type of policy can help students understand that timeliness is important, but it also recognizes that there may be times when life can get in the way of students being able to successfully complete a task on time.

As you work on developing your late and missed work policies, we encourage you to reflect on your goals and consult with colleagues and students to discuss the possible intended and unintended consequences of your policies. As you grapple with questions such as "How will you handle late work?" and "In what circumstances will you accept late work?" stay focused on the course learning goals and how your policies may support or distract from these goals.

Academic Integrity Policies

It is important to include academic integrity policies on the syllabus. Although most, if not all, students know that copying and pasting from the Internet and looking at another student's test are unacceptable and dishonest behaviors, students may not fully understand that other actions such as discussing a test with friends who have not yet taken the exam or submitting the same paper in two different classes are also considered dishonest behaviors. As a result, many students may engage in what are referred to as *unintentional dishonest actions* because they don't fully comprehend what it means to uphold academic integrity (Belter & du Pré, 2009). Thus, one of the primary goals of an academic integrity policy is to provide students with a solid understanding of what is and what is not acceptable behavior. Clearly articulate what it means to engage in academically honest work.

You can also, in an academic integrity policy, explain why honest actions really matter and describe consequences for dishonest actions. It is important to note that policies that list consequences, even if severe in nature, will often not make much of an impact on whether students plagiarize or cheat (McCabe, Butterfield, & Trevino, 2012). Thus, although it is still important to communicate this information to students, consequences should not be the focus of the policy. Rather, research has shown that other factors such as students perceiving their professor to be caring and respectful and expectations that students will engage in honest work have more of an impact on whether students will engage in honest or dishonest actions (McCabe et al., 2012). Thus, an academic integrity policy statement that communicates that you care about integrity and respect in the classroom is a more effective approach. Here is the academic integrity policy from the sample syllabus (additional policy examples can be found on pages 157–158 in the "Important Policy Information" section of the Appendix):

> Academic integrity benefits everyone in our community. It not only helps you reach the real goal of this class—learning—but also allows for the college and program to be perceived positively by others. When students are dishonest, they lose out on valuable learning that will help them perform well in their career. It can also negatively affect all of the students in the program and at the institution by creating negative mind-sets that may result in fewer outside learning opportunities for students. Academic dishonesty is any attempt by a student to gain academic advantage through dishonest means or to assist another student with gaining an unfair advantage. Academic integrity is important regardless of whether the work is graded or ungraded, group or individual, written or oral. Dishonest acts can result in a failing grade on an assignment, a failing course grade, and/or an official code of conduct charge being filed.

There are several strategies that can help increase academic honesty. First, teach students about academic integrity and the rules of citation , since the primary reason that students plagiarize is because they do not know the rules. This can be done in a variety of manners, through an online module, an in-class presentation, or a visit to the library or writing center. Second, create assignments that showcase early on who is having issues with citations and research. Make sure that these assignments are worth small point values but build up to a larger assignment (e.g., find one source and summarize it in one page with a citation). Also, when you scaffold a large paper like this, it takes away the procrastination factor to some degree, which is the second reason students plagiarize. The third strategy to increase academic honesty is to talk to students about their writing voice (or "authorial identity," as Elander, Pittam, Lusher, Fox, and Payne [2010] explored in their research). The third reason that students plagiarize is to impress you, the professor, and we can get around this by stressing how important it is for them to be heard throughout their paper, and how at this point in their career they are just looking to throw their penny into the pond—just their two cents on the topic. It will take the pressure off, and it is hoped students will feel more confident in their writing ability.

So, then, what about cheating? Bernardi, Baca, Landers, and Witek (2008) confirmed that some actions by professors can dissuade cheating, such as spreading students out in the classroom on test day, scrambling the test questions on different versions of the test in the classroom, increasing classroom supervision on test days, and changing test questions between semesters. Another important aspect is to clearly define what academic misconduct is. Take for instance a professor who assigns an online test for the first time. The students have been studying together and created a StudyBlue deck of electronic flashcards based on the study group's efforts. When it's time to take the online test, the students weren't given directions about what resources they could or could not use, so many chose to refer back to the flashcards. Some even used the text from the flashcards, word for word. Now three students are in trouble for cheating. How could this have been avoided? We can all agree that the study group was a great activity for the students to engage in, but using the product of the study group looks like collusion. To avoid situations such as the one described, professors can provide guidance and instruction on what is and is not appropriate behavior when taking an online test. Being concrete with students about what academic misconduct looks like on the front end will only save you time and hassle on the back end.

Behavior and Conduct Policies

Every college or university will have a code of student conduct that describes appropriate and inappropriate behaviors. The goal, of course, is to ensure that student behaviors support rather than distract from the student learning experience. This is an area of the syllabus where many faculty have a long list of dos and don'ts in terms of behaviors, often emphasizing certain behaviors that the professor finds to be particularly unacceptable. Although communicating our expectations is important, we need to think about the messages we want to send to our students. Instead of listing inappropriate behaviors, what if we instead focused on appropriate behaviors? This approach would send a message to our students that we expect them to behave appropriately and that we really care about creating a productive learning environment. Referencing the college's or university's code of student conduct instead of trying to replicate it in the syllabus is also recommended. Consider the following simple, yet productive, example related to behaviors that was used in the sample syllabus (see the "Important Policy Information" section on page 157 in the Appendix):

> To foster a productive learning environment, the college requires that all students adhere to the Code of Student Conduct, which is published in the college catalog and on the website.

A global approach versus a specific one to conduct policies is recommended, because when we list some of the appropriate behaviors and not others, we can unintentionally minimize the importance of the behaviors we didn't list. If we try to include all of the behaviors outlined in the code of conduct, we can let this begin to take over our syllabus, creating a legalese type of document.

Behaviors related to safety need special attention on the syllabus. For example, courses with a laboratory component may need to have additional rules or policies in place because of safety concerns. Although we want to bring attention to the policy, we want to consider how our students will receive and respond to the policy. For example, a policy that uses all capital letters and an exclamation point such as "NO FOOD and NO DRINKS in the LAB!" may make your students feel like you are yelling at them. Consider the following example as an alternative description of the policy:

> For your safety: Eating and drinking are not allowed in the lab. Please do not bring any food or beverages into the lab. We will be working with hazardous materials throughout the term. Eating or drinking during lab puts you and your classmates at increased risk of accident and injury from breakage or toxins. You will be asked to remove any food or beverage you bring into the lab.

Even when strict policies are needed, we will want to consider how we communicate these policies. As safety is obviously a primary concern, we may want to draw special attention to these policies by using a different color font or larger font.

RESOURCES AND STRATEGIES FOR SUCCESS

As faculty, it is our job to challenge and support our students. The syllabus communicates the challenge via the learning outcomes and assignments. However, the support piece is often not fully communicated in the syllabus. Some supports such as our office hours and the textbook resources are typically included, but other essential resources (e.g., tutoring support) are often not incorporated into syllabi. Doolittle and Siudzinski (2010) found that only 7% of the syllabi reviewed included information on support services. We believe this is a missed opportunity. The syllabus is a perfect place to communicate to students that there are many resources available as they embark on this learning journey. In other words, it is important to communicate to students that they will be supported as they strive to successfully meet the course learning outcomes.

Learning Resources

One of the primary resources in a class is the textbook. We are reminded by Collins (1997) that high school students borrowed their books, so if you are teaching first-year students, you might want to provide students with information about where to rent or purchase the required textbook and inform them about the online resources that typically accompany textbooks, especially if you will be requiring students to purchase access to the online supports. If you have placed the book in the campus library's reserved section, you should list this here as well, as many underserved students may have financial trouble acquiring the book during the first few weeks of class or acquiring it at all (Collins, 1997).

You can also use the syllabus to share video links that will assist students with using and taking full advantage of resources that they will need throughout the semester. For example, including links to brief screencasts on technology tools such as the learning management system, Dropbox or Google Docs, publisher tools, and the online library databases can be very helpful to students. Students will likely be appreciative of these efforts.

Let's not forget that we, the faculty of their courses, are one of the most important resources for our students. Thus, it is important that students know how to get in touch with us and know when we are available to meet with them. This is why we include our contact information and office hours in our syllabi. Even when we include this information, many students do not come to our office hours. Perrine, Lisle, and Tucker (1995) conducted an interesting study on the role of the syllabus in increasing the likelihood that students will access support. Their findings, based on an experimental study, indicated that adding just six words—"Please come and talk to me"—significantly increased students' willingness to seek help with a variety of problems, including having trouble understanding the textbook, getting a low grade on the first exam, and thinking about dropping the course. Six words were all it took to make a significant difference.

Consider providing a brief table or list of the primary campus resources in your syllabus. For example, inform students about the resources offered at the library, learning center, and counseling department. Remember, we are teaching the whole student, and many students might not be aware of these resources. Include contact information such as the website, phone number, and location. It can also be helpful to provide links in the syllabus to websites, making it very easy for students to find information on resources. Some campus learning centers have suggested syllabus inserts for their resources, such as the following:

> I encourage you to utilize the Center for Student Learning's (CSL) academic support services for assistance in study strategies, speaking and writing strategies, and course content. They offer tutoring, Supplemental Instruction, study strategy appointments, and workshops. Students of all

abilities have become more successful using these programs through-out their academic career and the services are available to you at no additional cost. For more information regarding these services please visit the CSL website.

By providing information that is specific to the course, we can increase the likelihood of students accessing resources as needed. Drawing on Collins (1997), we can see clearly that it is one thing to write,

> The Writing Center is located in Jones Library, first floor and can help with writing issues.

It is quite another thing to write,

> Tutors in the Writing Center on the first floor of Jones Library have met with me and understand my expectations for the major writing assignments in this course. They are prepared to review drafts or works in progress in-person by appointment, which can be made at www .joneslibrarywritingcenter.com/appointments.

Study Tips: How to Be Successful in This Course

If we view the syllabus as an opportunity to map out the learning path for our students, it makes sense that we would also want to include a section on study tips. Students do not always engage in the most effective study strategies. In fact, students often spend much of their study time on activities such as rereading and highlighting that will probably not lead to high levels of learning. McGuire (2015) argued that this is in part due to the fact that students focus on studying instead of learning. If the goal is learning, students would be more inclined to use strategies that result in long-lasting understanding. Students can make better use of their time and have more powerful results if they use learning strategies such as testing themselves using practice quizzes or flashcards and teaching others (Harrington, 2016). By including several research-based study strategies, you can help ensure that your students will know which study strategies to use to meet with success. McGuire (2015) noted, "If you teach students how to learn, and give them simple, straightforward strategies to use, they can significantly increase their learning and performance" (p. 2). Many students find the tips in "The Best Way to Study/Learn (According to Research!)" section on page 155 in the Appendix to be incredibly valuable; here you will see several study tips that students can use to meet with success.

In addition to providing students with strategies to assist them with learning the course content, you may also want to consider including a section on "academic etiquette" or how to effectively engage with the greater university and professional community. For instance, you could provide information on e-mail etiquette. Here is an example of information on e-mail and phone etiquette you may want to include on your syllabus:

> E-mail etiquette tips: Communication is an essential skill. As a college student, you want to build your professional identity. Make a good impression with your professors and staff by sending messages that are professional in nature.
>
> - E-mail communication: Use formal conventions of letter writing when composing e-mail:
>   - Include appropriate greetings such as Dear Professor Thomas.
>   - Remind them who you are and which class you are in. This is John Smith from your PSY 101 class that meets on Tuesdays and Thursdays at 11:00 a.m.
>   - Briefly describe the purpose of the e-mail. I have a question about next week's reading assignment, and I would like to see if I can meet with you sometime during your office hours between 1:00 p.m. and 3:00 p.m. tomorrow.
>   - Include an appropriate closing and identifying signature every time. You can set your e-mail account to put automatic signature information on all outgoing e-mail that includes your full name and contact information.

Providing students with tips on how to be successful in the course will likely result in positive outcomes. This approach can increase student motivation and ultimately achievement levels.

CHAPTER SUMMARY

In the end, policies and resources are meant to encourage students' success. Reflecting on the purpose and potential consequences, positive or negative, of our policies is important. How we write our policies and how we engage students with those policies and resources will likely play a significant role in our student outcomes. Here, more than anywhere else in the syllabus, language and tone really matter. We need students to understand why we have enacted the policies we have by emphasizing our desire for them to be successful in our course and in college.

REFERENCES

Belter, R. W., & du Pré, A. (2009). A strategy to reduce plagiarism in an undergraduate course. *Teaching of Psychology*, *36*, 257–261.

Bernardi, R. A., Baca, A. V., Landers, K. S., & Witek, M. B. (2008). Methods of cheating and deterrents to classroom cheating: An international study. *Ethics and Behavior*, *18*(4), 373–391.

Chen, J., & Lin, T. (2010). Class attendance and exam performance: A randomized experiment. *Journal of Economic Education*, *39*(3), 213–227.

Collins, T. (1997). For openers . . . an inclusive course syllabus. In W. E. Campbell & K. A. Smith (Eds.), *New paradigms for college teaching* (pp. 79–102). Edina, MN: Interaction Books.

Crede, M., Roch, S. G., & Kieszczynka, U. M. (2010). Class attendance in college: A meta-analytic review of the relationship of class attendance with grades and student characteristics. *Review of Educational Research*, *80*(2), 272–295. doi:10.3102/0034654310362998

Doolittle, P. E., & Siudzinski, R. A. (2010). Recommended syllabus components: What do higher education faculty include in their syllabi? *Journal on Excellence in College Teaching*, *20*(3), 29–61.

Elander, J., Pittam, G., Lusher, J., Fox, P., & Payne, N. (2010). Evaluation of an intervention to help students avoid unintentional plagiarism by improving their authorial identity. *Assessment and Evaluation in Higher Education*, *35*(2), 157–171.

End, C. M., Worthman, S., Mathews, M. B., & Wetterau, K. (2010). Costly cell phones: The impact of cell phone rings on academic performance. *Teaching of Psychology*, *37*(1), 55–57. doi:10.1080/00986280903425912

Gump, S. E. (2013). The cost of cutting class: Attendance as a predictor of success. *College Teaching*, *53*(1), 21–26.

Guskey, T. R. (2004). Are zeros your ultimate weapon? *Principal Leadership*, *5*, 31–35.

Harrington, C. (2016). *Student success in college: Doing what works!* (2nd ed.). Boston, MA: Cengage Learning.

Hutcheon, T. (2017). Excellence in teaching essay: Technology bans and student experience in the college classroom. *Society for the Teaching of Psychology*. Retrieved from http://www.teachpsych.org/Excellence-in-Teaching-Blog/5068179

Kent, C. (2016). To solve the skills gap in hiring, create expectations in the classroom. *The Chronicle of Higher Education*. Retrieved from http://www.chronicle.com/article/To-Solve-the-Skills-Gap-in/235206

McCabe, D. L., Butterfield, K. D., & Trevino, L. K. (2012). *Cheating in college: Why students do it and what educators can do about it.* Baltimore, MD: John Hopkins University Press.

McGuire, S. Y. (2015). *Teach students how to learn: Strategies you can incorporate into any course to improve student metacognition, study skills, and motivation.* Sterling, VA: Stylus.

Moore, R. (2005). Attendance: Are penalties more effective than rewards? *Journal of Developmental Education, 29*(2), 26–30.

Padilla-Walker, L. M. (2006). The impact of daily extra credit quizzes on exam performance. *Teaching of Psychology, 33*(4), 236–239.

Perrine, R. M., Lisle, J., & Tucker, D. L. (1995). Effects of a syllabus offer of help, student age, and class size on college students' willingness to seek support from faculty. *Journal of Experimental Education, 64*(1), 41–52.

Rubin, S. (1988). Professors, students, and the syllabus. *Graduate Teacher Program Handbook.* Board of Regents, University of Colorado. Retrieved from http://www.colorado.edu/ftep/sites/default/files/attached-files/ftep_memo_to_faculty_10.pdf

Sana, F., Weston, T., & Cepeda, N. J. (2013). Laptop multitasking hinders classroom learning for both users and nearby peers. *Computers and Education, 62,* 24–31.

Slattery, J. M., & Carlson, J. F. (2005). Preparing an effective syllabus: Current best practices. *College Teaching, 53*(4), 159–164.

St. Clair, K. L. (1999). A case against compulsory class attendance policies in higher education. *Innovative Higher Education, 23*(3), 171–180.

Wasley, P. (2008). The syllabus becomes a repository of legalese. *The Chronicle of Higher Education: The Faculty.* Retrieved from http://www.chronicle.com/article/The-Syllabus-Becomes-a/17723/

Wood, T., & Madden, S. (2014). Suggested practices for syllabus accessibility statements. Retrieved from kairos.technorhetoric.net/praxis/tiki-index.php?page=Suggested_Practices_for_Syllabus_Accessibility_Statements

5

DESIGN CONSIDERATIONS

*A*LTHOUGH CONSIDERING COURSE CONTENT is critical when you are developing a syllabus, the way in which this content is communicated is also important. Tone and the overall organizational structure have been found to affect students' perception of the course and the instructor (Harnish & Bridges, 2011). This can affect students' motivation and ultimately academic achievement, as students who have higher levels of motivation typically achieve at higher levels (Walker, Greene, & Mansell, 2006; Waschull, 2005). In addition, when a syllabus is presented in a way that is engaging and well organized, students are more likely to attend to this important document and find the information they need to meet with success.

TONE

Tone is an incredibly important consideration when you are developing your syllabus, and it affects students' motivation. Designing a motivational syllabus requires you to take a close look at how the information about the course is being communicated to students. Put yourself in the position of student for a moment, and consider a syllabus from one of your own courses. Imagine you have signed up for the course and open the course management system to find the syllabus has been posted. You read it eagerly to learn more about the course and what to expect this semester. As a student, how might you respond to the following questions about that syllabus from your class, knowing nothing about the course or the instructor except what is contained in the posted syllabus?

- What is your first reaction? How motivated or excited are you about the course?
- What is your perception of the professor and the course?
- Do you have a clear understanding of what you will learn and how you will learn it?
- Do you expect to be both challenged and supported this semester? What do you expect to be particularly challenging? What supports are available to you?
- Do you plan to refer to this syllabus regularly throughout the course? Why or why not?

After thinking about your responses (or, more important, how your students would likely respond) to these questions, is this what you want? In other words, is your syllabus communicating the messages you want to send to your students? Does it provide students with the information they need in a way that is encouraging and exciting? Is it likely that your syllabus is sparking student interest and engagement in your course? Does it accurately reflect your teaching approach and style? If you are uncertain about any of these questions, ask a trusted colleague to read your syllabus from the point of view of a student and then give you responses to the previous questions.

Lang (2015) argued that the syllabus is an opportunity for you to share your excitement and passion for the course with your students. Unfortunately, many syllabi have a negative tone, especially those that emphasize rules and policies more so than learning. Shifting the tone of a syllabus from negative to positive can have a significant, positive impact on motivation and learning. As you think about the tone of your syllabus, take a moment to consider what Ken Bain (n.d.) described as a promising syllabus: "a syllabus that makes promises rather than demands, inviting students to a deliciously provocative intellectual or artistic feast" (para. 1). This invitational approach can really make a difference in terms of motivation. In fact, there are some very simple, yet powerful strategies we can use to improve the tone in our syllabi. For example, language matters. It is important that we consider our word choices. In addition, adding explanations and images can also set a positive tone, motivating and inspiring students to engage with us and the course content.

LANGUAGE

Language is powerful. The way in which we write and the words we use affects how the message is received. Let's start by thinking about first, second, and third person. Many syllabi are written in the third person, with phrases such as "the professor will" or "students will be able to." What if instead you shifted to first and second person, using "I" and "you" language? This approach would be more personal, and as a result, students would probably feel more engaged and connected. Thus, the tone of the syllabus can be moved in a more positive direction by using first- and second-person language. It is, after all, a personal document for you and your students. The sample syllabus in the Appendix has numerous examples of how first- and second-person language can be used in a syllabus. For example, on the first page of the syllabus, you'll see it says, "Please reach out to me!" (see page 151). The "Learning Outcomes" section (see page 152) starts by stating, "Here's what you will be able to do after successfully completing this course," and in the "Teaching Philosophy" section (see page 153), "I" and "you" language is used throughout.

The power of modifying the language by changing a few words was demonstrated in a study by Harnish and Bridges (2011). In this study, 172 students were randomly assigned to a friendly or unfriendly syllabus condition. The friendly version had statements such as "I welcome you to contact me outside of class and student hours" and "I hope you actively participate in the course," whereas the unfriendly version had statements such as "If you need to contact me outside of office hours, you may e-mail me" and "Come prepared to actively participate in this course" (Harnish & Bridges, 2011, p. 323). Note that both messages were generally positive, but you can see how the friendly version was more personal and encouraging. After reviewing the syllabus, students answered survey questions about the professor and the course. Despite there being fairly minor language differences, there were several significant findings. Specifically, the students in the friendly condition viewed the professor as more approachable and more motivated to teach the course. Interestingly, the students in the friendly condition also thought the course was going to be less difficult than those students in the unfriendly condition did. Although the first two findings about approachability and motivation are desirable, this last finding does raise some concerns about students possibly misinterpreting approachableness for easiness. This can be problematic, as students who perceive the class to be less difficult may exert less effort and as a consequence may not learn as much in the course. However, another possible explanation is that the approachableness of the professor increases students' belief in their ability to successfully complete the course because they believe their professor will be there to support them on their learning journey. In other words, the clear communication of support may make it more likely that students will perceive the class to be "doable." When we use our syllabus to communicate to our students that they will be challenged as well as supported, we will likely increase their motivation.

Another important issue relates to positive language versus negative language. For example, instead of talking about academic misconduct, discuss integrity and honor. Research has found that there is less cheating at colleges and universities with honor codes as compared to colleges and universities that do not have honor codes (McCabe & Butterfield, 2012). On the basis of this research, the emphasis on the importance of integrity and establishing a culture where honesty is valued increases honest actions among all members of the community.

Sometimes our well-intentioned efforts to help students understand what is and is not acceptable behavior can negatively affect student motivation and learning. For example, syllabi that contain an endless list of behaviors that students should not engage in such as using mobile devices for nonacademic reasons and arriving to class late send a message that the professor is expecting students to misbehave. Students are not as likely to connect with a professor if they don't think the professor believes in them. Another example is when professors draw attention to a particular policy that they believe to quite important by using bold or capital letters. Using all capital letters, bolded print, or numerous exclamation points to communicate these policies magnifies the negative message. Agger and Shelton (2017) pointed out, "In the electronic age, the use of all capital letters or bold writing connotes yelling and not just emphasis" (p. 365). Similarly, a long list of behaviors that students should avoid, even if bold or capital letters were not used, could result in the same interpretation by students. A more positive approach would be to focus on appropriate behaviors rather than inappropriate ones. For example, you may want to indicate that you expect students to uphold the academic integrity of the class and to engage in behaviors that are consistent with your college's code of conduct and that foster a learning-focused environment. Research has found that when positive language versus punitive language is used, students find the professor to be more approachable (Wasley, 2008). Small language changes can have a significant, positive impact on students' actions; your relationship with students; and, most important, their learning.

The complexity of the language also matters. Presenting content in easier-to-understand language increases the likelihood that students comprehend the information we are sharing. Mayer (2009) discovered that students learned more when multimedia slides presented content using conversational language. Research has also shown that we are more likely to understand and recall information presented using a narrative approach. In an interesting study conducted by Hillier, Kelly, and Klinger

(2016), it was found that articles using a narrative writing approach were more likely to be cited than articles using the expository writing approach. In other words, professionals were more likely to use research when the article was written using a narrative approach versus a scientific one. The primary difference between the expository or scientific approach and the narrative approach is that the expository or scientific approach primarily communicates facts, whereas the narrative approach is designed to tell a story and evoke emotion. It makes sense then that students would also be more likely to understand and use a syllabus that is written using easy-to-understand terminology. To put this research into practice, you might want to consider using the syllabus as the mechanism to tell the story of the course. Stories have a beginning, a middle, and an end. Using backward design, you would tell the story of the class via the syllabus that starts with the end of the story and clearly communicates the goals or learning outcomes of the course. You would then describe the journey of how to achieve the goal by using a narrative approach, explaining the "why" and "how" of in- and out-of-class activities. Stories have long been associated with high levels of learning (Egan, 1985; Lordly, 2007). Thus, a storytelling approach to the syllabus can set the stage for higher levels of learning.

RATIONALE

In addition to the language used to list content, rules, and expectations, explanations can also add to a more positive tone. Unfortunately, Metzler, Rehley, and Kurz (2013) (as cited in Chick, 2014) found that most syllabi do not accurately give students an understanding of what will transpire during class or the rationale behind the learning activities. Palmer (2017) emphasized the importance of transparency when developing a syllabus. When students understand how you will run your class and the reasons for doing so, they will often be more willing to become active participants and be engaged in the learning process. Addressing the "why" behind the learning activities is a way to demonstrate to students that you care about their learning. These explanations can be quite helpful to students, assisting them to see the steps along the learning path you have mapped out to help them successfully achieve the course learning outcomes. Sharing the reason behind the learning activities also increases relevancy. Relevancy signifies meaning, and students want to engage in tasks that they perceive to be meaningful and important. Wlodkowski (2008) noted that relevancy is one of the most effective ways to quickly increase student motivation. Let's look at an example. On the one hand, if you require your students to take quizzes and you don't provide a reason for doing so, students may interpret the quizzes negatively, perhaps viewing them as busy work, as a way to "catch" them when they don't do their work, or as work that is more typical of the high school setting and not meaningful in the college setting. On the other hand if you share that you give quizzes because of the research on the testing effect (Roediger & Karpicke, 2006), students will be more likely to interpret your actions as being supportive in nature. Providing the evidence and rationale behind the learning task can help your students see the value and purpose of the task. In the "Assignment Details and Grading Rubrics" section of the sample syllabus (see the Appendix, pages 165–175), you'll see that a rationale for each assignment is provided. Here is one example from the sample syllabus (see the "Quizzes" section in the Appendix, page 174):

> Practicing retrieval is a very effective learning strategy. In fact, researchers have found that testing yourself is one of the best ways to learn (Roediger & Karpicke, 2006). To maximize your learning experience, you will be taking a quiz on every chapter. Quizzes are online. You can take each quiz up to three times (lots of retrieval practice!), and the highest score will count. These are called formative assessments—they are designed to help you learn.

Similarly, you could explain how group work and presentations will help students develop soft skills such as communication and collaboration, which are highly valued by employers (Robles, 2012). In addition, you can link the activities back to the overall course learning outcomes, as this is another powerful way to help students see the value and meaning of the learning tasks. By clearly sharing the rationale for why you selected the learning tasks, you will likely increase student motivation. Here is an example of how you could communicate the importance of and rationale behind a group project:

> As you know, one of the course learning goals is to be able to practice interpersonal and leadership skills essential in a diverse, global society. Interpersonal and leadership skills are also highly valued by employers. This group project will give you the opportunity to develop these important skills while also building your content knowledge.

The same is true for class and institutional policies. Providing a brief explanation of the reasons behind your policies helps students understand the rationale and need for these policies. You'll see several examples of rationales being provided in the "Important Policy Information" section in the sample syllabus (see pages 157–158 in the Appendix). Here is one example (see the "Late Work/Missed Exam Policy" section on page 158 in the Appendix):

All Students Are Expected to Complete Learning Tasks on Schedule

It is important to stay on track with your assignments; not only will this help you feel less stressed, but it is also an important skill you will need in your career. Being able to meet deadlines and juggle many tasks are important career and life skills. Thus, you will need to complete all quizzes, exams, and assignments according to the schedule. However, I recognize that personal circumstances may at times make it difficult or impossible to complete a learning task on schedule. If you have a personal situation that prevents you from completing a task on time, you will need to discuss this with me prior to the due date if possible or as soon as it becomes possible so that we can come up with a plan. Reading assignments can be submitted PRIOR to class in the learning management system if you will be absent. Extensions are at my discretion. If an extension is provided, it is important to know that the format of the exam or the assignment may be modified.

This approach shows our students that we care deeply about learning and want to create an environment where learning is the focus. Students often respond favorably when we take the time to share the "why" behind our policies and teaching approach.

IMAGES AND GRAPHICS

Research has shown that everyone with vision is a visual learner (Goswami, 2008). In other words, learning is increased when images are used (Mayer, 2009). In psychology, this is referred to as the *picture superiority effect*, which basically means that our memory for pictures is better than our memory for words (McBride & Dosher, 2002). Knowing the important role of images in learning, many of us use a variety of visual aids when we teach. In fact, many of us spend a considerable amount of time thinking about how visual tools such as images, charts, and graphs can best help us communicate our content via lectures. We also carefully examine and evaluate the visual features in textbooks. However, many of us do not transfer this use of images to our syllabus. Most syllabi are text only, with few, if any, images. In essence, visual images are an underutilized tool in the syllabus.

Visual tools can be used in the syllabus to help students easily see and take in important information about the course. Nilson (2007) suggested using visual images to "complement and supplement" text in the syllabus, noting that "visuals communicate the structure of and interrelationship among the topics to be covered and the abilities students need to learn" (p. 13). More specifically, graphics can be used to communicate work flow and connections between concepts or clearly illustrate steps or actions needed (Nilson, 2007; Sauer & Calimeris, 2015). Visual tools can also help us organize the material in a visually effective format. The value of Smart-Art, a free tool found in Microsoft Word and PowerPoint, is that it provides us with a way to visually package syllabus content, often showing students the connections or relationships between tasks or topics (Sauer & Calimeris, 2015). Biktimirov and Nilson (2003) pointed out that graphics in a syllabus can also model effective communication strategies for students, demonstrating how different tools can be used to present information in a clear and effective way.

Graphics that illustrate learning sequences or steps of a project can also make it easier for students to understand the required tasks. For example, SmartArt can be used to communicate what students need to do before, during, and after class. This is illustrated in the sample syllabus in the section titled "Your Learning Experience" (see the Appendix, page 156, and Figure 5.1).

Likewise, simple tools can also be used to communicate work flow for an assignment. For example, a chart or table could be used to show students the steps needed to complete an assignment. Figure 5.2 shows an example of a flowchart for a group presentation assignment. You'll notice that the group work components of the project are shaded to help students see how different parts of the process are to be completed independently or collaboratively with group members.

Figure 5.1. Your learning experience.

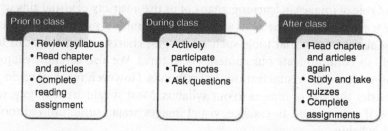

Figure 5.2. Group presentation assignment flowchart.

Step 1 (INDIVIDUAL WORK) Find research articles on the topic to share with group members.
Step 2 (GROUP WORK) Review articles from all group members and select an article for the presentation (must be approved by me).
Step 3 (INDIVIDUAL WORK) Write a summary of the research article (will be given an individual grade).
Step 4 (GROUP WORK) Discuss the research article, ensuring that all members of the group have a strong understanding of the research.
Step 5 (INDIVIDUAL WORK) Create a visual summary of the article (i.e.,PowerPoint) using research-based multimedia principles (will be given an individual grade).
Step 6 (GROUP WORK) Share presentations with group members, using ideas and information from individual members to create a PowerPoint presentation that will be used on the day of the presentation. Support all members with preparing for the presentation.
Step 7 (INDIVIDUAL WORK) Practice the entire presentation so that you are prepared to present the entire presentation by yourself, as you won't know what part you will be assigned to present until the day of the presentation. Reach out to group members for support as needed (will be given an individual and group grade).

Images and graphics not only assist us with taking in content but also motivate and inspire us. According to research conducted by Sauer and Calimeris (2015), students who were presented with a graphic syllabus indicated higher levels of excitement to take a course (43%) as compared to students who were presented with a traditional syllabus that did not contain graphics (18%). Adding a course-related photograph to the first page of your syllabus can draw students into the course. Consider the differences between the first pages of the two syllabi shown in Figure 5.3. Which would be more likely to motivate and engage you to read the entire syllabus and also suggest a more engaging course?

Photos can also be used in other sections of the syllabus. For instance, consider adding your photograph next to your teaching statement. Your photograph can add a personal element to the syllabus and the course, helping students feel connected to you prior to the start of the semester. This can be particularly useful in online courses. Adding a face to a name is helpful. This is illustrated in the "Teaching Philosophy" section in the sample syllabus (see the Appendix, page 153).

Figure 5.3. Two contrasting syllabi examples.

Middlesex County College
Educational Psychology
PSY 226-02
Meets on Tuesdays 9:30 a.m. – 12:00 p.m., BH 203

Professor: Dr. Christine Harrington
Charrington@middlesexcc.edu
732.548.6000
Office Location: Center I
Office Hours: Mondays 9:00 a.m. – 11:00 a.m. and 1:30 p.m. – 4:30 p.m.
Thursdays 1:00 p.m. – 2:00 p.m. and 3:30 p.m. – 4:30 p.m.

Pre-requisite: PSY 123

This course provides an overview of learning, motivational, and developmental theories with a focus on their application to the field of education. Educational research addressing the powerful role of the educator, effective teaching strategies, and curriculum decision making are discussed. Theory and research based practices to reach all learners in an educational environment are emphasized.

Learning Outcome:

Here's what you will be able to do after successfully completing this course:

1. Identify and discuss learning, motivational, and developmental theories with a focus on their application to the field of education. (Bloom's taxonomy: remembering and understanding) LO1

2. Describe the various educational research methods and apply this knowledge to evaluate the role of the educator. (Bloom's taxonomy: understanding, applying, evaluating) LO2

3. Determine best classroom and instructional practices in education. (Bloom's taxonomy: applying, analyzing, evaluating) LO3

4. Integrate theory and research to develop and implement a lesson plan related to educational psychology. (Bloom's taxonomy: creating) LO4

As you can imagine, these are important skills you will need as a future educator. The knowledge and skills gained in this course will help you meet with success in future courses, such as the Educational Field Experience. For example, the lesson planning experience you gain in this course will help you write more effective lesson plans in your practicum courses. As you know, this course is just one of the many educational courses you'll need to take to graduate. This course will help you develop a strong foundational knowledge in theories, research, and educational concepts so that you can apply this knowledge in a variety of educational situations and settings.

MIDDLESEX COUNTY COLLEGE

Welcome to

Educational Psychology!

PSY 226-02

Meets on Tuesdays 9:30 a.m. – 12:20 p.m. BH 203

Professor Contact Information: Please reach out to me!

Dr. Christine Harrington
charrington@middlesexcc.edu; 732.548.6000
Office Location: Center I

Office Hours: Mondays 9:00 a.m. – 11:00 a.m. and 3:30 p.m. – 4:30 p.m.
Thursdays 1:00 p.m. – 2:00 p.m. and 3:30 p.m. – 4:30 p.m.

Table of Contents:
Course Information 2-3
Campus Support and Policies 3-5
Course Outline 6-9
Grading Information 9-10
Assignments and Rubrics 10-47
Reading Assignment Questions 18-23

Note. Photo by Tom Peterson. Reprinted with permission.

Images can also be used to add clarity. For instance, inserting a photograph of the textbook cover into the syllabus can assure students that they have purchased the correct edition of the textbook. This simple strategy can reduce the number of questions that students often ask about the textbook (see Figure 5.4).

Charts or graphs can also be used to help students better understand specific components of the syllabus. For example, a graph could be used to help students better understand the grading distribution for the course.

Figure 5.4. Textbook image sample.

Note. Reproduced with permission (www.cengage.com/permissions).

A pie chart, for example, is a great way to visually show the weighting of assignments and how they count toward a final grade. In a research study conducted by Sauer and Calimeris (2015), 100% of students who reviewed a syllabus that used a pie chart to communicate the grading distribution indicated that they understood how their final grade would be determined, as compared to only 73% of the students who reviewed a traditional syllabus that did not include a pie chart. These results indicate that the pie chart helped students understand the weighting of assignments (see Figure 5.5).

This idea of making the syllabus a more visual document is not new; professionals such as Nilson (2007) have been advocating for the use of graphics in the syllabus for some time now. Researchers have found that graphically organizing content is more effective than using an outline format (Robinson & Kiewra, 1995). Research has also found that students respond more favorably to syllabi with images. Specifically, in an experimental study conducted by Harrington and Gabert-Quillen (2015), students were randomly assigned to an image or no-image syllabus condition. The images for the Lifespan Development syllabus consisted of three photographs depicting different stages of life, a photograph of the textbook, and a pie chart illustrating the grading system. Results indicated that students in the syllabus with images conditions used more positive words to describe the syllabus (89.4%) as compared to students who were in the syllabus without images conditions (76.5%). However, there were no significant differences between the images and no-images conditions in terms of student perception of the professor or course. It

Figure 5.5. Grading distribution.

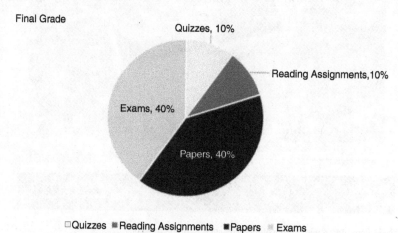

is important to note that both versions of the syllabi in this study, with and without images, used other visually effective tools such as charts and SmartArt to describe the learning process. Although the data on images in syllabi are limited, it is unlikely that including an image will have a negative impact on the tone of the syllabus. Rather, it is more likely that an image may help send an inviting message and add clarity to information being communicated. Biktimirov and Nilson (2003) argued that adding graphic elements to a syllabus also increases the likelihood that students will recall important information about the organization and structure of the course. On the basis of these findings, we need to think about how we can use visual tools and images to add clarity and make our syllabus content more inviting.

Although images and graphics add a lot of value for most students, it is important to remember that these tools can make it more difficult or even impossible for students who are blind or have visual impairments to take in the information. We need to consider accessibility when creating documents or other resources, and this obviously includes the syllabus. Alternative text needs to be provided when images or other graphics are used. Using graphics as an additional tool rather than the only or primary method of communication is advised. There are many ways you can determine if there are accessibility issues in the documents you create. One example is the Accessibility Checker that can be found in Microsoft Word.

ORGANIZATION AND CLARITY OF INFORMATION

Has a student ever asked you a question about an assignment or due date and your response was "It's in the syllabus"? Many professors get quite frustrated when they take a considerable amount of time and effort to develop a comprehensive syllabus and their students do not seem to use it. Although students' inquiries may sometimes be due to forgetting to check the syllabus, they may also be a result of not being able to easily find the information when they do look for it. In general, we give up pretty quickly if we aren't able to find the information we need right away. According to Haile (2014), most us spend 15 seconds or less actively engaged on a web page, abandoning the search if not successful. Students will likely spend more time looking for information on the syllabus than they would on a website because they want to be successful and may need the information they are seeking to successfully accomplish a learning task. However, it is still human nature to become frustrated when we cannot find information we need.

It is important for us to recognize that it may take students longer than we think for them to find the information they need. This is particularly true with syllabi that look like legal contracts and are long and wordy. The information may be in the syllabus but could be buried in the middle of a ton of text. Likewise, what we perceive to be straightforward and clear may not be to the student. This is in part due to the fact that as experts, we find it easier to make accurate inferences when needed (Hrepic, Zollman, & Rebello, 2004). In other words, as experts, we can more easily deduce what is meant even if it is not explicitly stated. Students, however, may not be able to do this or may come to inaccurate conclusions. Thus, although it is the student's responsibility to carefully use important class resources such as the syllabus, it is also important for us as faculty to create a syllabus that is well organized, clear, and straightforward. Drawing our students' attention to the most important parts of the syllabus and using a clear organizational structure will help students make the most of this important resource and find the information they need to meet with success.

On the basis of eye-tracking research, Nielsen (2006) discovered that we use an F pattern when reading websites, with our attention being given first to the content at the top of the page and then down the left side of the page, periodically scanning across the page when something grabs our attention. Although this research was conducted using webpages and not syllabi, these scanning behaviors are likely similar, especially when students are viewing the syllabus electronically on a screen. On the basis of these findings, Nielsen (2006) suggested that the most important content be discussed first, with powerful, informational words being used in headings and bullet points.

Headings are a simple, yet effective organizational tool used in many learning resources, including syllabi. Research has shown that students are able to take in information more efficiently and effectively when meaningful headings are used (Hyönä & Lorch, 2004). The headings form the organizational structure of the document. In some cases, we will need to use the headings modeled in departmental or institutional templates that have been provided to us. In other cases, we may have the freedom and flexibility to create the headings and organizational structure. Reviewing our heading choices to be sure we have maximized the use of subheadings and have created a well-organized syllabus is a worthwhile investment of our time. While we are engaged in this task, we may also want to think about the best titles for our headings. Using questions rather than statements as headings might be one way to improve our syllabi. Research has found that students are more actively reading when searching for an answer to a question. For example, the Survey-Question-Read-Recite-Review

(SQ3R) reading method has been shown to be quite an effective strategy, increasing comprehension for material read (Artis, 2008). Other learning resources such as textbooks often begin the chapter with the learning outcomes posed as questions. Why not also use this approach in the syllabus? For example, instead of using "Learning Outcomes" as the heading, perhaps we could use the question "What Will You Learn in This Class?" or "What Will You Know or Be Able to Do as a Result of Taking This Class?" as the heading. If you like the idea of the question but do not want to lose the official terminology, a good compromise could be to use both the formal terminology and the question in the heading; for example, "Learning Outcomes: What Will You Know or Be Able to Do as a Result of Taking This Class?" The sample syllabus that is located in the Appendix has several examples of heading and subheadings. For example, in the "Course Content Areas" section of the sample syllabus (page 153), the three main topics are in bold within a table format. Another example can be found in "The Best Way to Study/Learn (According to Research!)" section (page 155) where numbering and bolded font are used to draw our attention to the main study strategies students should use to increase learning.

Simple tools such as font features can also help organize content. For example, attention will be drawn to headings with a larger font size or fonts that are bolded or in color. Similarly, using a shaded box or shape can be helpful from an organizational perspective (Biktimirov & Nilson, 2003). In the "Course Outline" section of the sample syllabus (see pages 159–163), you'll see that the learning objectives for each day are in bold and italics. In addition, group work is in all capitals to draw students' attention to the fact they will need to come to class prepared and ready to participate in their group.

From an organizational perspective, it can be helpful to provide students with links rather than provide all of the information they need within the actual document. When you provide links to resources, websites, and policies, then your syllabus becomes what Afros and Schryer (2009) referred to as a "web-mediated" syllabus. But Afros and Schyrer (2009) warned against too many links, which might overwhelm the student. In a research study conducted by Grigorovici, Nam, and Russill (2003), it was found that students had a more positive impression of the instructor when viewing a syllabus that had either no links or three links as compared to a syllabus that had three links that then linked out to three additional links. Thus, we caution against having too many links. An example of using a link in a syllabus can be found in the "Registrar Withdrawal Information" section of the sample syllabus (see the Appendix, page 158). Here, you will see that the link goes to deadlines related to withdrawing from the course.

An advantage of using a linked approach here is that you won't have to be concerned about writing an incorrect date on your syllabus.

Nielsen (2006) suggested that the most important content should come first. However, determining what information belongs on the front page or at the top of a page can be challenging. The placement of the information does, at some level, communicate its importance, and prioritizing what is most important is an essential task. For example, if our contact information is buried toward the end of the syllabus, this probably would communicate that we are not very interested in our students reaching out to us for assistance. If, however, this information is on the first page, students would likely believe we are interested in supporting them, and as a result, they may be more likely to reach out to us when needed. You'll notice that the professor's contact information is on the first page of the sample syllabus (see the Appendix, page 151). Likewise, think about how differently a student would perceive a document that begins with all of the specific requirements of the course or policy information as compared to a syllabus that begins with an engaging overview of the course. If, as Bain (n.d.) suggests, we are going to view the syllabus as an invitation to our course, then it is probably important that we provide an overview and describe how we plan to teach the course at the beginning of the syllabus. Remember, this type of information can excite and engage students, and it is hoped that having this information appear in the beginning of the syllabus will encourage students to continue reading the rest of this important document.

Give students the information they need first at the beginning of the syllabus. Introducing students to the course and helping them get to know you are most critical at the start of the semester and therefore at the start of the syllabus. Rubrics for assignments, however, are not needed immediately. Although it is important for students to know that this important information is contained in the syllabus, it is not necessary for them to read this section of the syllabus carefully at the very beginning of the course. Thus, rubrics are best suited for the end of the syllabus or even in an appendix. Students can then turn their attention to the rubrics when they begin working on the assignment.

As you develop your syllabus, if you note it is getting long, you may want to consider using some organizational aids to help students navigate through the content. Adding a brief table of contents on the front page is another organizational strategy that can make it easier for students to find the information they are seeking. You may even want to link the table of contents to the various sections of the syllabus for ease of use. If you use a link, students will be able to click on the section and go directly to that page in the syllabus (see Figure 5.6).

Just as you wouldn't expect your students to read an entire textbook the first week of class, it may not be important for students to read the entire syllabus at the start of the semester. However, it is important for students to become familiar with the information contained within the syllabus so that they know when to refer back to the syllabus. The syllabus, like the textbook, is a resource for the course. It is important to draw attention to the parts of the syllabus that students need to attend to right away. A table of contents is one way to help orient students to the type of information contained in the syllabus and will help students find the information they need.

LENGTH

What is the optimal length for a syllabus? If it's too short, it may not provide students with all of the information they need. If it's too long, students may become overwhelmed and not even read it. How does the length of the syllabus affect students' perception of the course? As noted previously, syllabi were at one time very brief, sometimes just one or two pages.

One reason why syllabi were probably shorter many years ago was the concern about the environment, printing costs, and the difficulty of typing additional material. Today, with most students having access to technology at their fingertips, this may no longer need to be a concern. In a large-scale study of over 75,000 college students, Dahlstrom and Bichsel (2014) found that 86% of undergraduates reported owning a smartphone, and

Figure 5.6. Sample table of contents.

Table of Contents
Course Overview 2
Policies 3
Assignments 4–5
Grading 6
Course Outline 7–8
Grading Rubrics 9–11
Reading Assignments 12–14

approximately half had their own tablet. Many students opt to access their syllabus via their phone, tablet, or computer, and as a result, many professors no longer provide hard copies of their syllabus to their students. This online access also makes it easier to use color and images in the syllabus. Thus, a short syllabus may no longer be needed.

Another reason that syllabi were previously shorter in duration was that the focus was on teaching rather than learning. A syllabus created from a teaching-focused paradigm can be brief and may include just a course description and brief outline. However, the paradigm shift from teaching to learning (Barr & Tagg, 1995) has resulted in faculty thinking about more ways to use the syllabus as a tool to promote learning and success. As Palmer, Wheeler, and Aneece (2016) emphasized, a learning-focused syllabus provides students with all of the information they need to meet with success. To accomplish this task, more details will be needed, and thus, syllabi will likely be longer.

A longer syllabus gives you the space to use more creative ways to share information and connect and engage students. It may take up more space to use a graph, chart, or SmartArt feature, but these visual tools can help organize the content. The use of white space in documents can also improve readability (Hart, 2008). It is much easier to use all of the visual tools to help organize content when we are not restricted to a certain number of pages. As previously discussed, graphics can enhance students' understanding of and engagement with the course. Shifting away from the view of the syllabus as a brief, informative document toward the idea that the syllabus can become a course manual or map that serves to motivate and inform can lead to increased levels of student success. In essence, the syllabus becomes the main course resource, mapping out the path for success. Your students will likely appreciate a visually effective, comprehensive syllabus.

Although there are only a few research studies investigating syllabus length, the consistent finding that seems to emerge is that longer is better than shorter. Jenkins, Bugeja, and Barber (2014) found that students appreciate it when more detailed information is included in the syllabus. In another study conducted by Saville, Zinn, Brown, and Marchuk (2010), it was also found that students had more positive perceptions of faculty who had a longer syllabus (6 pages) as compared to a shorter syllabus (2 pages). As many professors have syllabi that are sometimes 10 to 15 pages in length or even longer, Harrington and Gabert-Quillen (2015) investigated much longer syllabi in an experimental study. Results indicated that students in the medium syllabus group (9 pages) perceived the course and the professor more positively than those in the short syllabus (6 pages) or long syllabus (15 pages) groups. Students in the medium (9 pages) or long (15 pages) syllabus groups believed their professors cared more and would be more helpful and were more motivated to take the course as compared to students in the short (6 pages) syllabus group.

Faculty have two main choices when creating a syllabus for their course: include the basic information and provide the assignment details when needed later in the course or package all of the assignment details within the syllabus. When the first approach is used, it can be challenging for students to quickly find the information they need to successfully complete the assignments. Faculty often use different sections of the course learning management system. For instance, some faculty may set up their course by modules, whereas others may use only a few features such as a file sharing space or announcements. As a result, students are faced with finding assignment information in many different places for their different courses. Barlow (2017) noted that students can become frustrated with this process and spend valuable time looking for assignment details rather than working on the assignment itself. This can be particularly challenging when students find themselves with faculty who approach these organizational tasks differently. In these cases, students must use different navigational techniques to find the information they need in each course they are taking.

Packaging all of the course materials such as assignment details and rubrics into the syllabus centralizes important information, making it easier for students to locate needed information. In a research study conducted by Harrington and Gabert-Quillen (2015), 66% of students indicated that their preference would be to have all of the assignment information included in the syllabus as opposed to having a syllabus with the basic information and then receiving the assignment details later on in the semester. This study provides further evidence for students' preference for a longer syllabus. Students seem to appreciate having more detailed information about resources and assignment expectations early on in the semester. This approach goes beyond traditional views of the syllabus and truly uses the syllabus as a motivational tool that maps out the learning path for students.

CHAPTER SUMMARY

When you develop your syllabus, how you communicate content matters. For example, the language that we use can make a big difference in terms of student motivation. Using a positive tone and first- and second-person language is recommended. In addition, as instructors we can help our students see the connection between assignments and the course-level and program-level learning outcomes. Clearly communicating the key content in a visually effective manner is essential. The messages matter more than the length. Incorporate images or graphics as appropriate to add clarity and to engage your students. An organizational structure that will be easy for students to follow and understand is also critical. It's not enough to include the information; it is also important that the students can easily find the information they need. Time spent thinking about the design of your syllabus will be time well spent, as it will result in a syllabus that motivates and informs students.

REFERENCES

Afros, E., & Schryer, C. F. (2009). The genre of syllabus in higher education. *Journal of English for Academic Purposes, 8,* 224–233. doi:10.1016/j.jeap.2009.01.004

Agger, B., & Shelton, B. A. (2017). Time, motion, discipline: The authoritarian syllabus on American college campuses. *Critical Sociology, 43*(3), 355–369. doi:10.1177/0896920515595844

Artis, A. B. (2008). Improving marketing students' reading comprehension with the SQ3R method. *Journal of Marketing Education, 30*(2), 130–137.

Bain, K. (n.d.). The promising syllabus. The Center for Teaching Excellence at New York University. Retrieved from http://kenbain.site.aplus.net/promising-syllabus.pdf

Barlow, R. (2017, June). *Dogfooding a syllabus (Times four).* Presented at the Lilly Teaching and Learning Conference, Bethesda, MD.

Barr, R. B., & Tagg, J. (1995). From teaching to learning: A new paradigm for undergraduate education. *Change, 27*(6), 12–25.

Biktimirov, E. N., & Nilson, L. B. (2003). Mapping your course: Designing a graphic syllabus for introductory finance. *Journal of Education for Business, 6,* 308–312.

Chick, N. (2014). What's in your syllabus? Vanderbilt University Center for Teaching. Retrieved from https://cft.vanderbilt.edu/2014/01/whats-in-your-syllabus/

Dahlstrom, E., & Bichsel, J. (2014, October). *ECAR study of undergraduate students and information technology, 2014* (Research report). Louisville, CO: ECAR.

Egan, K. (1985). Teaching as story-telling: A non-mechanistic approach to planning teaching. *Journal of Curriculum Studies, 17,* 397–406. Retrieved from http://www.educause.edu/ecar

Goswami, U. (2008). Principles of learning, implication for teaching: A cognitive neuroscience perspective. *Journal of Philosophy of Education, 42*(3–4), 381–399.

Grigorovici, D., Nam, S., & Russill, C. (2003). The effects of online syllabus interactivity on students' perception of the course and instructor. *Internet and Higher Education, 6,* 41–52.

Haile, T. (2014). What you think you know about the web is wrong. *Time*. Retrieved from http://time.com/12933/what-you-think-you-know-about-the-web-is-wrong/

Harnish, R. J., & Bridges, K. (2011). Effect of syllabus tone: Students' perceptions of instructor and course. *Social Psychology of Education: An International Journal, 14*(3), 319–330.

Harrington, C. (2016). *Student success in college: Doing what works!* (2nd ed.). Boston, MA: Cengage.

Harrington, C., & Gabert-Quillen, C. (2015). Syllabus length and use of images: An empirical investigation of student perceptions. *Scholarship of Teaching and Learning in Psychology, 1*(3), 235–243.

Hart, G. S. (2008). *Typography 101B: The role of white space in making words readable*. Retrieved from http://www.geoff-hart.com/articles/2008/typography-101B.htm

Hillier, A., Kelly, R. P., & Klinger, T. (2016). Narrative style influences citation frequency in climate change science. *PLoS ONE, 11*(12), e0167983. doi:10.1371/journal.pone.0167983

Hrepic, Z., Zollman, D., & Rebello, S. (2004). Students' understanding and perceptions of the content of a lecture. *AIP Conference Proceedings, 720*(1), 189–192. doi:10.1063/1.1807286

Hyönä, J., & Lorch, R. F. (2004). Effects of topic headings on text processing: Evidence from adult readers' eye fixation patterns. *Learning and Instruction, 14*(2), 131–152. doi:10.1016/j.learninstruc.2004.01.001

Jenkins, J. S., Bugeja, A. D., & Barber, L. K. (2014). More content or more policy? A closer look at syllabus detail, instructor gender, and perceptions of instructor effectiveness. *College Teaching, 62*(4), 129–135.

Lang, J. (2015). The 3 essential functions of your syllabus, part I. *The Chronicle of Higher Education*. Retrieved from http://chronicle.com/article/The-3-Essential-Functions-of/190243

Lordly, D. (2007). Once upon a time . . . Storytelling to enhance teaching and learning. *Canadian Journal of Dietetic Practice and Research, 68*(1), 30–35.

Mayer, R. E. (2009). *Multi-media learning* (2nd ed.). New York, NY: Cambridge University Press.

McBride, D. M., & Dosher, B. (2002). A comparison of conscious and automatic memory processes for pictures and word stimuli: A process dissociation analysis. *Consciousness and Cognition: An International Journal, 11*(3), 423–460.

McCabe, D. L., & Butterfield, K. D. (2012). *Cheating in college: Why students do it and what educators can do about it*. Baltimore, MD: John Hopkins University Press.

Nielsen, J. (2006, April). *F-shaped pattern for reading web content*. Retrieved from https://www.nngroup.com/articles/f-shaped-pattern-reading-web-content/

Nilson, L. B. (2007). *The graphic syllabus and the outcomes map: Communicating your course*. San Francisco, CA: Jossey-Bass.

Palmer, M. (2017, June). *The science of transparency.* Plenary presentation at the Lilly Teaching and Learning Conference, Bethesda, MD.

Palmer, M. S., Wheeler, L. B., & Aneece, I. (2016). The evolving role of syllabi in higher education. *Change, 48*(4), 36–46.

Robinson, D. H., & Kiewra, K. A. (1995). Visual argument: Graphic organizers are superior to outlines in improving learning from text. *Journal of Educational Psychology, 87*(3), 455–467. doi:10.1037/0022-0663.87.3.455

Robles, M. M. (2012). Executive perceptions of the top 10 soft skills needed in today's workplace. *Business Communication Quarterly, 75*(4), 453–465.

Roediger, H., & Karpicke, J. D. (2006). Test-enhanced learning: Taking memory tests improves long-term retention. *Psychological Science, 17*(3), 249–255. doi:10.1111/j.1467-9280.2006.01693.x

Sauer, K. M., & Calimeris, L. (2015). The syllabus evolved: Extended graphic syllabi for economics courses. *Journal of Economics and Economic Education Research, 16*(1), 135–148.

Saville, B. K., Zinn, T. E., Brown, A. R., & Marchuk, K. A. (2010). Syllabus detail and students' perceptions of teacher effectiveness. *Teaching of Psychology, 37*(3), 186–189. doi:10.1080/00986283.2010.488523

Walker, C. O., Greene, B. A., & Mansell, R. A. (2006). Identification with academics, intrinsic/extrinsic motivation, and self-efficacy as predictors of cognitive engagement. *Learning and Individual Differences, 16*(1), 1–12. doi:10.1016/j.lindif.2005.06.004

Waschull, S. B. (2005). Predicting success in online psychology courses: Self-discipline and motivation. *Teaching of Psychology, 32*(3), 190–192. doi:10.1207/s15328023top3203_11

Wasley, P. (2008). Research yields tips on crafting better syllabi. *The Chronicle of Higher Education, 54*(27), A11.

Wlodkowski, R. J. (2008). *Enhancing adult motivation to learn: A comprehensive guide for teaching all adults* (3rd ed.). San Francisco, CA: Jossey-Bass.

6

EVALUATING THE SYLLABUS

REFLECTION AND EVALUATION ARE considered essential practices in the field of education. As educators, we will often reflect on which teaching strategies and approaches are best helping students achieve the course learning outcomes, but we may not always take time out to reflect on the overall design and structure of our course. In an extensive research review conducted by Hogan, Rabinowitz, and Craven (2003), the power of reflection was emphasized, with research showing that expert teachers more regularly engage in reflective practices. Although there are many benefits associated with reflection, Ferraro (2000) noted, "The primary benefit of reflective practice for teachers is a deeper understanding of their own teaching style and ultimately, greater effectiveness as a teacher" (p. 4). This is not surprising, as reflection often results in our making modifications to our course design or teaching methods in order to better align with the learning outcomes and improve student learning.

Teaching scholars have called us to incorporate reflective practices in our pedagogy (Brookfield, 2015; Rendón, 2009) and our practice (Bain, 2004). Reflection related to all aspects of teaching is critical, but reflecting on the overall course design is particularly important. Students are more likely to achieve at higher levels when professors expertly design and teach courses. This was illustrated in a quasi-experimental study conducted by Stewart, Houghton, and Rogers (2012). In this study, students taking a course that was developed using Fink's taxonomy of significant learning experiences and used active learning approaches reached higher levels of achievement of the student outcomes for the course when compared to students taking a course where Fink's taxonomy was not used.

By using backward design and focusing on learning outcomes when developing your course and syllabus, you will be targeting your attention on student learning, answering the call from Barr and Tagg (1995) to shift from a teaching focus to a learning focus. Research has shown that a learner-centered teaching style is connected to improved learning conditions and achievement (Opdenakker & Van Damme, 2006). Designing a course with the end in mind means that we are carefully considering how assessments and learning tasks will help students learn and achieve the course goals. This focus on learning increases the likelihood of achievement.

Langer (1993) conducted extensive research on mindfulness and its connection to learning. She defined *mindfulness* as "a state of mind that results from drawing novel distinctions, examining information from new perspectives, and being sensitive to context" (p. 44). Approaching teaching and the creation of our syllabi from a mindful state, where we look at our syllabi through multiple lenses and are concerned about how each piece is perceived and understood by students, is recommended. As we engage in the process of redesigning our course and syllabus, it is a perfect time to engage in reflection. As learning is an ongoing process, this process of reflecting and improving is also ongoing. In other words, it is important for us to continue to reflect even after the redesigned syllabus is complete. The process of reflection continues while teaching the course and upon completion of a course. This way, we can continually make improvements to the syllabus and course.

There are a variety of strategies that you can use to engage in reflection and evaluation related to the syllabus. Getting feedback on your syllabus in several ways and at different points during the creation process is recommended. For example, you can engage in self-reflective practices, ask students for feedback, and seek feedback from faculty colleagues within and outside of your discipline. Researchers have found that a variety of self-assessment and other assessment approaches can lead to improved lessons and learning, though feedback from experts was the most impactful in a study with preservice teachers (Ozogul, Olina, & Sullivan, 2008). It is therefore recommended that you use several different reflection approaches.

Engaging in self-assessment is a good place to start. Research has shown that self-assessment can be beneficial, especially when standards or criteria are used during this process (Ross & Bruce, 2007; van Diggelen, den Brok, & Beijaard, 2013). When you evaluate your syllabus, you may find it helpful to use checklists and rubrics as a guide during this process. The syllabus checklist (see Figure 6.1) and syllabus rubric, a more in-depth evaluative tool (see Table 6.1) are tools that can be particularly helpful if you are redesigning your syllabus or course.

Figure 6.1. Syllabus checklist.

Questions to Consider

Essential Components

Course Information
- Course name and number
- Course description
- Purpose and value of course
- Course learning outcomes and connection to program learning outcomes
- Learning objectives for modules, units, or classes
- Overview of course content, including topics
- Location, times, days
- Textbooks and supplemental readings
- Calendar of activities

Instructor and Campus Support Information
- Professor name
- Office location and hours
- Contact information: phone, e-mail address
- Welcome statement and teaching philosophy
- Information on available campus resources
- Tips for success

Assignments and Grading Information
- Grading policy, scale, and weighting of assignments toward final grade
- Assignments and descriptions
- Rationale for assignments and link back to course learning outcomes
- Grading details and rubrics
- Course outline with due dates

Policy Information
- Late and missed work policy
- Attendance policy
- Academic conduct policy, including academic integrity policy
- Disability policy

Essential Elements

Tone
- What is the tone of the syllabus?
- Is it personal and engaging?
- What emotional reaction do you have to this document?
- Do you have a sense of excitement about the course?

Value and Purpose
- Do you see the value of the course and understand its purpose?
- Are the learning outcomes clearly defined?
- How would you describe this course to someone?

Organization and Clarity
- Do you know what to do to meet with success and how to access help if needed?
- Is it well organized and easy to follow?
- Can you easily see what is expected of you?
- Were enough details provided?
- Does the syllabus provide you with a clear path to success?
- Were visual tools such as charts used to organize the information and clearly communicate information?

Perception of Professor
- How would you describe the professor based on this syllabus?
- Do you expect to be challenged and supported by the professor?
- Do you think the professor is excited to teach this course?
- Do you think the professor believes in you?
- Would you be likely to take courses offered by this professor?

Perception of the Course
- Would you be likely to register for this course?
- What did you like the most about the syllabus?
- What suggestions do you have to make the syllabus better?

Table 6.1
Syllabus Rubric

Part I: Essential Components
Please note that some information is either present or missing and cannot be eligible for exceptional credit. In these cases, the exceptional column box will be grayed out and the maximum score will be 1 instead of 2 for that category.

Essential Components	Missing (0)	Present (1)	Exceptional (2)	Total Score
Basic Course Information				
Course name and number				
Course description			Overview of the course includes not only content but also value and purpose of the course.	
Location				
Meeting dates and times				
Textbook and supplemental readings			Syllabus includes photo of textbook cover and/or link to purchasing information for textbook or to additional readings.	
Learning outcomes			Outcomes represent variable levels of learning at the course level and are aligned with Bloom's or Fink's taxonomy. Action verbs are used. Clear, measurable outcomes are stated. Learning outcomes are introduced with student-friendly language, such as "What will you be able to do as a result of this class?" Course learning outcomes are linked to program outcomes and skills needed in the career path.	

Essential Components	Missing (0)	Present (1)	Exceptional (2)	Total Score
Calendar of activities			Assignment due dates are clearly indicated on the calendar so students can visually see the workload. There is a clear overview of what students will be doing before, during, and after class. Sequence of learning activities are aligned to learning outcomes and assessments.	
Instructor and Campus Support Information				
Professor name				
Office location and hours (or best way to contact professor if part-time)				
Contact information: E-mail and/or phone				
Welcome statement and teaching philosophy			The statement communicates the professor's passion for teaching and the discipline. The professor shares beliefs about and approaches to teaching and learning.	
Information about the professor			The professor provides educational and professional background, making connections to the course.	
Tips for success			The professor provides students with specific study strategies, referencing the research behind the strategies.	

(Continues)

Table 6.1 (*Continued*)

Essential Components	Missing (0)	Present (1)	Exceptional (2)	Total Score
Information on campus resources			The professor encourages use of campus resources and includes phone, location, and/or links to offices such as Counseling and Career Services, Academic Advising, Registrar, Library, Learning Center and Tutoring Services, and Disability Services.	
Course Learning Outcomes				
Various levels of learning			Outcomes represent variable levels of learning at the course level and are aligned with Bloom's or Fink's taxonomy.	
Measurable outcomes			Action verbs are used. Outcomes are linked to assignments or assessments.	
Emphasis on learning			Importance is drawn to this section of the syllabus. Emphasis on learning is introduced with student-friendly language, such as "What will you be able to do as a result of this class?"	
Linkage to program outcomes and careers			Course is contextualized within the program and career path. Course learning outcomes are explicitly linked to program outcomes and skills needed in the career path.	

Essential Components	Missing (0)	Present (1)	Exceptional (2)	Total Score
Assignments and Grading Information				
Due dates for assignments				
Assignment information			Detailed, clear explanation of assignments is included.	
Rationale for assignments and linkage to outcomes			The purpose of each assignment is clearly articulated, noting the connection between assignments and course learning outcomes. There is an explicit explanation about how the assignment provides evidence of learning outcome.	
Formative and summative assessments			Summative assessments will provide evidence of achievement of learning outcomes. There is inclusion of several formative assessments for every summative assessment. Assessments are labeled as *formative assessment* or *summative assessment*, and feedback opportunities are described.	

(Continues)

Table 6.1 (*Continued*)

Essential Components	Missing (0)	Present (1)	Exceptional (2)	Total Score
Grading information for assignments			Grade is composed of several different assignments. Syllabus includes rubrics that explain how assignments will be graded. Weighting of assignment grades toward final course grade is identified. Grading scheme and final grade will reflect whether learning outcomes have been achieved, representing growth and not penalizing students for not mastering skills at the beginning of the semester.	
Overall grading scale for course			Syllabus includes visual graphic of how much assignments count toward the final grade.	

Essential Components	Missing (0)	Present (1)	Exceptional (2)	Total Score
Policy Information				
Academic conduct policy			Syllabus includes a positively phrased statement about professional behaviors (i.e., "All students are expected to engage in behaviors that foster a learning-focused environment and are consistent with the behaviors outlined in the code of student conduct.").	
Academic integrity policy			A positively phrased statement emphasizes the importance of integrity and defines honest and dishonest actions. Policy includes potential consequences for dishonest actions.	
Attendance or participation policy			The value of and expectations related to class attendance and participation are explained.	
Disability policy			Information about how to access accommodations is provided in the beginning of the syllabus and focuses on inclusion.	
Late and missed work policy			Policy language communicates the importance of timeliness with an understanding that exceptions may be needed and avoids high-level penalties that will likely result in failure.	
TOTAL SCORE FOR ESSENTIAL COMPONENTS				

(*Continues*)

Table 6.1 (*Continued*)

Part II: Essential Elements

Essential Elements	Needs Work (1)	Satisfactory (2)	Exceptional (3)	Score
Organization				
Emphasis on important points	All information appears to be of equal value.	Important information (i.e., learning outcomes) is given priority placement in the beginning of the syllabus.	Important information focused on learning appears before policy information. Attention is drawn to important points (larger fonts, visual images, arrows, etc.).	
Content flow	Syllabus lacks headings or other organizational tools.	Headings are used to identify sections. Course information such as learning outcomes and course content areas is listed before policy information.	Important information, especially information related to learning outcomes, is presented in the beginning of the syllabus. Sequencing of content emphasizes learning and is easy to follow. Organizational tools such as headings and a table of contents are used.	

Essential Elements	Needs Work (1)	Satisfactory (2)	Exceptional (3)	Score
Path to success	Syllabus lacks detail about how to meet with success in the course.	Information about how to be successful is provided within the syllabus but not explicitly discussed.	Syllabus provides specific information and statements about how to meet with success and achieve course learning outcomes. There are explicit connections between formative and summative assignments and assessments. Syllabus includes a visual map of what students need to do to learn.	
Visual appeal	There is little to no use of tools such as font size, color, or images.	Some tools such as larger font size or bolded text are used to visually organize content.	Visual tools such as images, charts, graphs, and SmartArt are used to enhance the visual organization and appeal, making the syllabus a more inviting document.	
Tone				
Positive, personal language	Statements assume that students will misbehave or not act professionally (e.g., "Don't plagiarize."). Language is not personal (i.e., "students," "professor").	Personal language is used. Some policies and statements are phrased positively.	Personal language is used (i.e., "you" and "I"). Statements are positively phrased, communicating belief in the student (e.g., "It is expected that we will all engage in academically honest behaviors.").	

(Continues)

Table 6.1 (*Continued*)

Essential Elements	Needs Work (1)	Satisfactory (2)	Exceptional (3)	Score
Motivation	Information in syllabus provides basic course information but does not present information in a motivational way.	Syllabus includes general statements about the value of the course.	Syllabus includes explicit statements about the professor's belief in the students to complete the challenging course tasks. Syllabus includes explanations about why students should be excited about the course and how this course can assist with goal achievement.	
Support	There is no mention of resources or encouragement of students to reach out for help.	Information on how to access support on campus or other resources for help with completing tasks is provided.	Statements that encourage students to reach out to professor or other supports are included (i.e., "Please come and talk with me."). Links and related information to helpful resources are included.	
TOTAL SCORE FOR ESSENTIAL ELEMENTS				

If you are in the process of redesigning your syllabus, you can begin by looking at your current syllabus to determine the areas of strength and the areas that need to be improved. This self-assessment activity will get you focused on the key elements of the syllabus and how effectively you have communicated this information. In addition, you can change other important factors such as tone and organization at the beginning of the redesign process. You can then use the syllabus checklist and syllabus rubric again during the revision process and after you have completed the redesign of your syllabus. By using the checklist and rubric to monitor progress and evaluate your final product, you will ensure that your syllabus includes all of the essential components of the course and that this information has been communicated in a productive way that engages and motivates your students.

Student feedback can also be incredibly useful. After all, the syllabus is a document that is being created for students. It therefore makes sense that you would be interested in how students perceive your syllabus. This can help you determine if you have been successful at communicating the messages you intended to send to your students. For example, students can provide valuable feedback on important factors such as tone, organization, amount and type of information, ease of use, and overall perception and value of the course. A study conducted by Scully and Kerr (2014) provides a great example of the meaningfulness of student feedback. In this study, it was found that student perception of workload was influenced by the clarity of assignment expectations and whether assignments were linked to learning goals. More specifically, students in this study were more likely to perceive the workload to be manageable when professors provided clear expectations about assignments. This study illustrates how student feedback can provide you with useful information that you can use to improve your syllabus.

You can gather formal and/or informal feedback from students. For instance, you could use an informal approach and ask students to review your syllabus and provide you with general feedback on the tone and perception of the course. A more formal approach would be to ask students to evaluate the syllabus using the syllabus checklist (see Figure 6.1) or syllabus rubric (see Table 6.1). Another option is to ask students to participate in a brief focus group where they discuss what they find useful or helpful and what they find confusing in the syllabus. A colleague teaching education-related courses may even be willing to use class time for a focus group of your syllabus if the evaluation process and related conversation is aligned with the learning outcomes of the course he or she is teaching. If this is not a possibility, you can reach out to psychology or other departments that have established protocols and procedures, and perhaps even built-in incentives, for having students complete surveys or focus groups outside of class time. If these opportunities already exist, you can find out if a syllabus review might be added to the options for students participating in research-related activities as a course requirement or extra credit opportunity. If you use a focus group approach, it is best to have a colleague serve as the facilitator and then provide you a written and verbal summary after the focus group. Students may not feel comfortable sharing their thoughts with you as their professor. It is also best if these approaches are used with students who have not taken your class so that their feedback is truly based on the syllabus and does not also focus on your teaching style. However, a student who has taken a course with you before might be more able to give you feedback on a whole new version of your course syllabus and pinpoint if it accurately describes what happens during the semester or reflects your attitude toward teaching through its tone (Calhoon & Becker, 2008). Whichever approach you use, you will likely want to get feedback from many students. As different students may interpret your syllabus in different ways, getting feedback from a large number of students will be more meaningful than relying on the opinions of just a few. Getting feedback from a large group of students means that it will be more likely that the feedback you receive will be generalizable to future students.

Peer feedback may also prove to be very helpful. Ross and Bruce (2007) noted that combining self-assessment with peer-assessment facilitates professional growth in educators. The best place to seek out peer feedback is your campus teaching and learning center. Most campuses have an office that specializes in supporting faculty in their teaching endeavors that has staff or faculty who may be able to provide insightful feedback on your syllabus. Some teaching centers regularly present workshops on creating learning-centered syllabi and have created tools such as rubrics to assess your syllabi using campus constructs and expectations (Smith, 2015). Teaching and learning centers may also offer a group approach to feedback where several professors submit syllabi, and the group members do a round-robin review of each other's syllabi. If your college or university does not have a teaching and learning center or the center does not offer services related to a syllabus review or evaluation, you can reach out to a colleague on campus. Most faculty are willing to assist a fellow colleague as he or she aims to improve teaching and learning practices, especially if you offer to reciprocate. You could seek out a few colleagues and use the round-robin approach just described. Daniels, Pirayoff, and Bessant (2013) found that peer collaboration positively affected teaching practices. Specifically, their research indicated that it was beneficial for faculty to participate in instruction cadres, where faculty observed one another and engaged in reflective dialogue. Although this research was focused on teaching practices in general, this could also work for syllabus and course design. In this case, faculty could work with colleagues from other disciplines as they develop their motivational syllabus based on backward design. Faculty could then provide feedback and suggestions to one another. As previously mentioned, this service may be offered through the teaching and learning center on your campus, but if this is not the case, you can reach out to colleagues and engage in this process informally. Providing your colleagues with the syllabus checklist (see Figure 6.1) and syllabus rubric (see Table 6.1) can be quite helpful. This way, your colleagues can use these tools to provide you with specific feedback on your syllabus.

The teaching and learning center is not the only office that could be helpful to you as you engage in the syllabus redesign process. Another office to visit is the student learning center, whose services are devoted to helping students learn. Professional staff will likely be able to help you see what parts of your syllabus will be helpful to students and what parts of the syllabus or course structure might be confusing or misleading. Professional tutors or learning specialists often work with students who are struggling academically, so they see firsthand many of the challenges related to the course and assignment expectations that students encounter. The student learning center staff is also in touch with really outstanding students, such as tutors or supplemental instruction leaders, who might be willing to also provide feedback on your syllabus. Getting feedback from students with different strengths and weaknesses will likely help you develop a syllabus that will work well for a diverse group of students. Another place to find assistance is the disability services office. Disability service providers can provide feedback and advice on the universal design of your course, helping you ensure that your syllabus and course are accessible to all and can also provide you with a suggested inclusive learning statement. Finally, education departments are an excellent resource. Faculty teaching in this department have pedagogical expertise and are often very willing to share their expertise and time to assist colleagues interested in improving their course. Even though education faculty are typically focused on elementary and secondary educational practices, the same course design principles apply in higher education.

In addition to the many ways you can seek support from colleagues on your campus, national supports may also be available. Many disciplines have professional organizations, and some of these professional organizations have teaching- and learning-focused divisions. For example, in psychology, the American Psychological Association is a national professional organization for psychologists, and there is a division focused on the teaching of psychology. This division is called the Society for the Teaching of Psychology. One of the projects or resources provided by this division is called Project Syllabus (Society for the Teaching of Psychology, n.d.). In addition to providing resources on how to develop a strong syllabus, Project Syllabus also allows faculty to submit their syllabus for a formal peer review. Syllabi submitted for this purpose are anonymously reviewed by psychology faculty peers. Feedback, typically from two reviewers, is then provided to you, and you can use this feedback to improve the syllabus you are developing for your course. A positive review can even result in your syllabus being shared on the website as an exemplar. Investigate whether your discipline has a similar service. If so, take advantage of the opportunity for peer feedback at the national level. If not, perhaps you can encourage your professional organization to consider adding this service.

CHAPTER SUMMARY

Engaging in intentional reflection and evaluation processes as you design or redesign your syllabus will lead to an improved document that will motivate your students and provide them with a clear learning map for your course. Using a combination of self-assessment and student and peer evaluation processes will likely lead to the best outcome. This process works best when you use a syllabus checklist (see Figure 6.1) or syllabus rubric (see Table 6.1). For additional guidelines or rubrics, see Palmer, Bach, and Streifer (2014); Slattery and Carlson (n.d.); or Smith (2015). Your students will appreciate and benefit from the time and effort you put into the redesign process. Students will have more positive impressions of you, as the professor, and of the course in general if you create a syllabus that has a positive tone and maps out the path to success. This can translate into higher levels of motivation and achievement (Harnish & Bridges, 2011; Palmer et al., 2014).

REFERENCES

Bain, K. (2004). *What the best college teachers do.* Cambridge, MA: Harvard University Press.

Barr, R. B., & Tagg, J. (1995). From teaching to learning: A new paradigm for undergraduate education. *Change, 27*(6), 12–25.

Brookfield, S. D. (2015). *The skillful teacher: On technique, trust, and responsiveness in the classroom* (3rd ed.). San Francisco, CA: Jossey-Bass.

Calhoon, S., & Becker, A. (2008). How students use the course syllabus. *International Journal for the Scholarship of Teaching and Learning, 2*(1), Article 6. Retrieved from https://doi.org/10.20429/ijsotl.2008.020106

Daniels, E., Pirayoff, R., & Bessant, S. (2013). Using peer observation and collaboration to improve teaching practices. *Universal Journal of Educational Research, 1*(3), 268–274.

Ferraro, J. M. (2000). *Reflective practice and professional development* (ERIC No. ED449120). ERIC Digest.

Harnish, R. J., & Bridges, K. R. (2011). Effect of syllabus tone: Students' perceptions of instructor and course. *Social Psychology of Education, 14*(3), 319–330.

Hogan, T., Rabinowitz, M., & Craven, J. A., III. (2003). Representation in teaching: Inferences from research of expert and novice teachers. *Educational Psychologist, 38*(4), 235–247.

Langer, E. J. (1993). A mindful education. *Educationalist Psychologist, 28*(1), 43–50.

Opdenakker, M., & Van Damme, J. (2006). Teacher characteristics and teaching styles as effectiveness enhancing factors of classroom practice. *Teaching and Teacher Education, 22*, 1–21.

Ozogul, G., Olina, Z., & Sullivan, H. (2008). Teacher, self, and peer evaluation of lesson plans written by preservice teachers. *Educational Technology Research and Development, 56*(2), 181–201. doi:10.1007/s11423-006-9012-7

Palmer, M. S., Bach, D. J., & Streifer, A. C. (2014). Measuring the promise: A learning-focused syllabus rubric. *To Improve the Academy: A Journal of Educational Development, 33*(1), 14–36.

Rendón, L. I. (2009). *Sentipensante (sensing/thinking) pedagogy: Educating for the wholeness, social justice, and liberation.* Sterling, VA: Stylus.

Ross, J. A., & Bruce, C. D. (2007). Teacher self-assessment: A mechanism for facilitating professional growth. *Teaching and Teacher Education, 23*(2), 146–159. doi:10.1016/j.tate.2006.04.035

Scully, G., & Kerr, R. (2014). Student workload and assessment: Strategies to manage expectations and inform curriculum development. *Accounting*

Education: An International Journal, 23(5), 443–466. doi:10.1080/09639284. 2014.947094

Slattery, J. M., & Carlson, J. F. (n.d.). Pointers for preparing exemplary syllabi. Retrieved from http://teachpsych.org/Resources/Documents/otrp/syllabi/ exemplary_syllabi.pdf

Smith, J. (2015). Crafting a learner-centered syllabus. Retrieved from https:// pastprof.wordpress.com/2015/10/19/crafting-a-learner-centered-syllabus/

Society for the Teaching of Psychology. (n.d.). Project syllabus description. Office of Teaching Resources in Psychology. Retrieved from http://teachpsych.org/ otrp/syllabi/index.php

Stewart, A. C., Houghton, S. M., & Rogers, P. R. (2012). Instructional design, active learning, and student performance: Using a trading room to teach strategy. *Journal of Management Education, 36*(6), 753–776. doi:10.1177/1052562912456295

Van Diggelen, M., den Brok, P., & Beijaard, D. (2013). Teachers' use of a self-assessment procedure: The role of criteria, standards, feedback and reflection. *Teachers and Teaching: Theory and Practice, 19*(2), 115–134. doi:10.1080/135406 02.2013.741834

7

USING THE SYLLABUS

THE SYLLABUS IS AN incredibly important document. Research has consistently shown that students report regularly reviewing this course document. In a study conducted by Smith and Razzouk (1993), 20% of the participants reported using the syllabus every day, and 57% of the participants reported using the syllabus at least once per week. Thus, most students are referring to this important resource at least once per week. That makes the syllabus one of the most important documents in the course and one that should be designed with careful attention to detail. Unfortunately, not all students take full advantage of this important document. One way to increase students' use of the syllabus is to include information that students value and need. When students view the content in the syllabus as meaningful and as an important resource, they will be more likely to use it throughout the semester. For example, students with a syllabus that contains detailed information and guidance about assignments would be more likely to regularly refer to the syllabus as compared to students who have a syllabus that contains only general information about the course. Thus, the nature of the syllabus will affect the frequency in which students use it throughout the semester.

Students will also be more likely to view the syllabus as an essential course resource if they fully understand its value and how it can be best used to support their success. As faculty, we can help students gain a better understanding of how best to use the syllabus. In other words, we can inform students that the syllabus is a resource that should be referred to regularly throughout the semester. For example, students can learn how to use the syllabus to understand the purpose and goals of the course, to prepare for class, and as an important resource when completing assignments.

Too often, the syllabus is a document that is focused on only at the beginning of the semester. Because the syllabus provides an overview of the course and outlines the expectations, it makes sense that students and faculty would spend more time focused on this document at the start of the course. The syllabus certainly serves as a useful tool that can help students become oriented to the course. Findings from a research study conducted with 19 instructors from a variety of disciplines indicates that the average amount of time spent on the syllabus during the first day of class was 26.6 minutes, with a range from 15 to 40 minutes (Thompson, 2007). How much time we spend on the syllabus, how we present the syllabus content, and the level of detail and emphasis we give to different sections of the syllabus communicates "our own orientation toward the syllabus and its role in the course" (Fornaciari & Dean, 2014, p. 708).

Although most faculty focus on the syllabus on the first day of class, the syllabus continues to serve as a useful resource throughout the semester, especially if you have packed it full of assignment details, rubrics, and information suggested throughout this book. As the instructor for the course, you can help students learn to appreciate the value of the syllabus throughout the semester, viewing it as an essential course resource, much like the textbook. There are three opportune times that you can use it: before the first day of class, the first day or week, and then periodically throughout the semester with purpose.

BEFORE THE FIRST DAY OF CLASS

Do you wait until the first day of class to disseminate the syllabus? Some faculty send a welcoming e-mail to their students with the syllabus attached. This is a great way for students to learn about you and the course before the semester even begins and provides an opportunity for you to build excitement about starting the course. In essence, the syllabus can be used to motivate and engage your students before they even meet you or their classmates. A research study conducted by Legg and Wilson (2009) showed that sending an e-mail to students prior to the start of the semester had long-lasting benefits. Specifically, students who received the e-mail prior to the start of the semester perceived the class more positively and had higher levels of motivation than those who did not receive the e-mail, even during the last week of the semester. It is important to note that students were randomly assigned to either receive an e-mail or not receive an e-mail and that the instructor was unaware of who received or did not receive the e-mail. The graduate assistant managed the e-mail and responses. Although this welcome e-mail did not include the syllabus, this study does provide evidence that reaching out before the semester has a positive impact on students. To our knowledge, we are not aware of any studies that investigated the impact of sending the syllabus to students prior to the start of the semester, but it seems likely that sharing this resource ahead of time would be useful to students. This would be particularly true with a motivational syllabus that conveys to the students that you care about their success in the course.

Sending the syllabus to students ahead of time allows students to review and digest course information on their own schedule and can reduce the amount of time needed in class to review the syllabus. However, as noted previously, the communication surrounding the syllabus is incredibly important. Let's take a look at the issue of length and student interpretation and perception of long syllabi. Research conducted by Harrington and Gabert-Quillen (2015) found that most students (66%) preferred a detailed syllabus; however, some students reported feeling overwhelmed by a long syllabus. Given this concern, sending your syllabus ahead of time without much of an introduction or explanation may not be advisable. Fortunately, there are a variety of approaches you can use to help you orient students to your syllabus and course, reducing the likelihood that students will feel overwhelmed.

One simple strategy is to include an introductory paragraph or two in the body of your e-mail that helps students focus on what is most important and explains that details about assignments are provided for their convenience but that it is not necessary to review all of this information at once. If using this approach, you can provide students with suggestions on how to review the syllabus. For example, you can tell them to review the syllabus in a way that will enable them to convey the primary purpose of the course to another student. You could even ask students to come to the first day of class with a one-paragraph summary of the course. Another approach might be to share only the first couple of pages that really emphasize the purpose and value of the course, informing students that details about the assignments and other expectations are forthcoming. To help students get excited about the course, you may even want to consider adding a student quote or two from evaluations from prior semesters, especially if students made mention of how the workload is manageable and the assignments are meaningful. In other words, adding some tips on how students can best review the syllabus and sharing other student experiences in the course can help students better understand the course and become motivated to begin.

Adding an audio or video element can be quite powerful when you share the syllabus prior to the start of the semester. This allows students to have access to your tone, affect, and perhaps facial expressions if a video is used. This is particularly important because nonverbal communication helps ensure messages are accurately received. One excellent approach is to use a screencast of the syllabus. This can be particularly useful in an online course, but it also has tremendous value in face-to-face classes. Screencast tools such as Screencast-O-Matic allow you to record narration and also capture whatever is on your screen. Imagine having your syllabus on the screen and then drawing attention to key components, especially content that students need to know at the start of the semester. In addition to visually focusing students' attention on key elements, your voice adds affect and clarity. Students will appreciate this online orientation to the syllabus and course and will be able to review it as needed throughout the semester.

The way we communicate matters as much as, if not more than, what we communicate. Thus, the tone connected to the verbal messages we send about the syllabus can be quite helpful to students. We all know that the same words can be communicated in very different ways, depending on tone and affect. By adding an audio or visual component to our communication, we can be more confident that students will accurately interpret our messages. Tools such as Adobe Pro or VoiceThread enable you to add voice clips to various parts of the syllabus, giving you the ability to explain assignments or inform students why a particular section of the syllabus is so important. To even further enhance the communication, consider using a webcam or other video tool. This way students will also have access to facial expressions and other nonverbal communication, which can help messages be received with increased accuracy and meaning.

Instead of focusing only on communication from you to your students, you can also think about how to engage students in a conversation with one another about the syllabus and course before the first day of class. One way to accomplish increased student engagement is to ask students to participate in an online discussion about the syllabus. Rovai (2002) pointed out that online discussions can be a very effective way to get students engaged with the course content, their classmates, and also with you, the instructor. An online discussion board gives students the opportunity to comment or ask questions about the syllabus. Using this approach may lead to students thinking more critically about the course content, as research has shown that critical thinking is more likely in online discussion as compared to in-person discussions (Kamin, Glicken, Hall, Quarantillo, & Merenstein, 2001).

By having students pose questions, you can determine what areas of the syllabus are not clear and provide additional clarifying information as needed. If you ask students to also share what most excites them about the course, you can get a good idea about their areas of interest and passion. You can then use this information throughout the semester, making connections between their interest areas and the course content.

SYLLABUS ACTIVITIES FOR THE FIRST DAY AND FIRST WEEK

Regardless of whether we share the syllabus prior to the start of class, most of us do distribute and go over the syllabus on the first day of class. However, the way in which we do this really matters. Unfortunately, many faculty read and review the entire syllabus, often taking a large portion of the first class period explaining the syllabus to the students. This approach will not likely lead to high levels of student engagement (Gannon, 2016), and depending on how much content is covered, it may well be difficult for students to take in all of the information. Rather than "covering" the syllabus, consider more active learning approaches that can familiarize students with the syllabus. This way, students will know the content contained within the syllabus and as a result will be able to determine when to refer back to this important document. Active approaches are also more likely to facilitate higher levels of learning and engagement.

The first day of class is arguably one of the most important days of the entire semester. We all know that first impressions matter, but did you know that students' impressions after the first day are predictive of their evaluations at the end of the semester? In a study conducted by Laws, Apperson, Buchert, and Bregman (2010), 384 undergraduate students from 14 different psychology courses were asked to evaluate their professor and course at the start and end of a semester. On the majority (11 out of 18) of survey questions, there were no significant differences found between responses given after the first day and during the last week of the semester. Thus, our interactions on the first day with students really matter. This is not a new finding. In 1977, Parish and Campbell found a significant correlation between evaluations from the first day of class and evaluations at the end of the semester. First impressions are long-lasting and are more powerful than other types of information students may have about a professor. Researchers have found, for example, that first impressions of professors mattered more than the professors' reputation in terms of later impressions (Buchert, Laws, Apperson, & Bregman, 2008).

What do students value on the first day of class? Bassett and Nix (2011) found that students care about the following class factors in respective order: course difficulty, professional information, structure and content of the course, procedural details, and personal information. Course difficulty includes how to do well in the course and how much work will likely be involved. This will help students balance the work of this course with their other courses and responsibilities. Professional information includes the grading schema, the professor's name, and how to refer to her or him. Structure and content of the course include the syllabus, course schedule, required readings, and preexisting knowledge needed to be successful in the course. Procedural details include policies and procedures of the sources. Personal information includes icebreakers and information about the professor.

It is important to note that personal information about the professor was expressed as more important in general education courses than in discipline-specific courses and was highly correlated to feelings of connectedness in instructor–student relationships (Bassett & Nix, 2011). Even if students rated personal information about the professor as less important than other components of the syllabus, research has shown that students who feel a greater sense of connectedness with the instructor tend to be more self-directed and self-efficacious in their learning (Creasey, Jarvis, & Knapnik, 2009).

So, what are the first-day vehicles to provide students with the information they want, set the tone for the entire semester, share the purpose and value of the course, clearly communicate expectations, and yet connect students with one another and the instructor? Gannon (2016) emphasized the importance of the first day of class activities being reflective of the rest of the class. In other words, if you will be using technology as a teaching tool, consider using technology as you review the syllabus. Thompson (2007) found that students were more likely to pay attention to syllabus discussions when technology was used and the syllabus was projected on the screen. Likewise, if you plan to use active learning strategies throughout the course, then start using these approaches on day one. Familiarizing students with the syllabus through active learning strategies works very well. Spending time engaging students in discussions related to course expectations is one worthwhile approach. This was illustrated in a study conducted by McGinley and Jones (2014), who found that students who had the opportunity to discuss perceptions and feelings about the course and the course goals and topics of interest had higher levels of caring and interest as compared to students who did not have this opportunity.

The value of icebreakers in establishing a sense of community has been long known. Weimer (2013) emphasized that getting students talking to one another and to you, their professor, is an important first-day goal. Recognizing the importance of facilitating a community of learners, faculty even incorporate icebreakers into online courses, and research has shown that icebreakers have value in the online learning environment too (Dixon,

Crooks, & Henry, 2006). However, some have argued that traditional ice-breakers that focus exclusively on students getting to know one another may not be enough, believing that icebreakers can accomplish more than just increasing comfort and establishing a positive learning environment. According to Anderson, McGuire, and Cory (2011), the primary goals of the first day of class are to get the attention of students, immerse students in the course content, begin skill development, and establish connections. Effective icebreakers can serve multiple purposes, tapping into course-specific content in addition to establishing a sense of belonging and connection. For example, Eggleston and Smith (2004) emphasized the importance of relevance to the class, advocating that icebreakers should be connected to the course content, and shared numerous examples of icebreaker activities that are specifically designed for psychology classes. The syllabus can easily be used in this way, incorporating course content into icebreaker activities.

Intermixing some typical icebreaker-type questions with some course-based questions so that students can get to know one another and delve into the syllabus can work well. For example, you can create questions such as "What learning objective does X assignment meet?" or "What's the purpose behind X assignment?" that target the course content. In addition, ask questions such as "What is something unique about yourself?" or "What are you most passionate about?" These questions can help students to tap into course content and also establish relationships. In other words, this type of icebreaker will allow students to dig into the syllabus, begin to get to know one another, and even develop skills that will be needed for group activities later in the semester.

There are several best practice options for using the syllabus in ice-breakers or active learning opportunities, including a syllabus quiz, news clip course introduction, round-robin activities, negotiation and collaboration exercise, brainwriting, reciprocal interview, and a Jigsaw Classroom Exercise (Aronson, Blaney, Stephan, Sikes, & Snapp, 1978) on the syllabus. These engaging and interactive approaches can increase students' attention to this important document (Thompson, 2007).

Syllabus Quiz

Quizzing has many benefits. Experimental research conducted by Roediger and Karpicke (2006) has demonstrated that students are more likely to retain information over longer periods of time when they practice recalling or retrieving content. Quizzing is an excellent way to engage students in practice retrieval, an important learning activity. McDaniel, Wildman, and Anderson (2012) conducted an experimental study in a college classroom setting and discovered that online quizzing, as compared to rereading content, led to higher levels of academic performance. In other words, testing yourself leads to higher levels of learning. This is commonly referred to as the "testing effect."

Another benefit of quizzing is the feedback that often follows. Feedback is one of the most powerful ways to learn (Taras, 2006). The importance of feedback was illustrated in a study conducted by Kim and Shakory (2017). Findings from this study revealed that feedback on quiz performance early in the semester was predictive of performance on the cumulative final exam.

Quizzes can also serve as accountability tools. Quizzes communicate to students that the related content is important to focus on and study. In an interesting study conducted by Stratton (2011), students were asked what professors should do to make it more likely that they will engage in academic tasks such as reading. One key response from the students was accountability; students indicated that they would put forth more effort and time if given a quiz. Gannon (2016) argued that in addition to holding students accountable for important content, a quiz on the syllabus can also familiarize students with the course in a low-stakes environment. Given the many benefits of quizzing, a quiz on the syllabus is an approach that can help students engage with this important document. Faculty development professionals have been suggesting the use of a syllabus quiz as a way to review the syllabus in a more active way for many years. For example, Glascoff (1984) described several purposes of the syllabus quiz over 30 years ago.

Many different variations of the syllabus quiz have been discussed in the scholarship of teaching and learning (SoTL) literature. Raymark and Connor-Greene (2002) experimented with a type of syllabus quiz that had students respond to hypothetical student scenarios according to the syllabus. A few examples of the hypothetical scenarios include "Steve had a medical emergency and he missed class. Now he asks you how that is going to affect his grade"; "Bill asks about the policy for assigning final grades (for example, whether they are based on a curve)"; and "Ann asks you to explain the purpose of the research participation points" (Raymark & Connor-Greene, 2002, p. 287). They found that students who completed the syllabus quiz did better on a later true–false quiz about syllabus content. It is important to note that they found that students who took their time on the initial quiz and took it more seriously did even better. As a result, Raymark and Connor-Greene (2002) suggested that the syllabus quiz count toward the final grade rather than as an extra credit opportunity so that students put forth high levels of effort.

Leslie Jo Sena (personal communication, March 2017) suggested giving the syllabus quiz during the second week of class, noting that this approach gives students time to review the syllabus at length and also starts the trend to have the syllabus be something that is discussed throughout the semester. Another advantage of this approach is that the add–drop period has typically settled down, meaning students who were added to the course late don't miss out on the benefit of this activity. Sena (personal communication, March 2017) noted the importance of reviewing the answers to the syllabus quiz in class and have the students self-correct. This duplicates the testing effect (Roediger & Karpicke, 2006) very early on in the semester, which is not only an important study strategy to indoctrinate first-year students into but also something that can be reinforced for students in their upper-division courses.

Guertin (2014) took a different approach, requiring students to earn a perfect score on an open-book, online syllabus quiz before being able to gain access to course information in the learning management system. Students can take the syllabus quiz as many times as needed to earn a score of 100% on the quiz. Guertin (2014) noted that students are able to recall syllabus content throughout the semester and beyond.

Although many faculty think of quizzes as independent learning activities, research has shown that group quizzing is beneficial in many ways. For example, Slusser and Erickson (2006) found that students who participated in collaborative testing were more likely to complete learning tasks such as reading outside of class and had more positive attitudes about learning as compared to students who did not participate in collaborative testing. Harton, Richardson, Barreras, Rockloff, and Latane (2002) also found that it was beneficial for students to participate in focused interactive learning activities that required students to first complete a quiz independently and then work in a group to discuss the quiz questions. Results of this study on both lower- and upper-class students indicated that students who participated in these activities outperformed students who did not participate in interactive learning activities. This was evidenced by higher grades on tests and students reporting that this activity helped them connect with other students (Harton et al., 2002). Although this research was focused on collaborative quizzing related to course content, many faculty have used an interactive group syllabus quiz to help familiarize students with the syllabus.

To use an interactive group syllabus quiz approach, students are assigned to work with approximately three to four other students. After receiving the quiz, students are asked to answer the questions and note the page number of the syllabus where they located the answer. Some faculty may choose to add a competitive element to this activity by giving a few extra credit points to the group that completes the quiz first, if all of their answers are correct. A modification of this approach is to have each student work with a partner and use polling questions that are projected onto the screen. In this approach, students answer the questions using their cell phones. A multiple-choice format works best with polling tools. In addition to having answer responses be specific content, you can also consider having the answers be page numbers on the syllabus where the content can be found. This latter approach emphasizes the role of the syllabus as a course resource. Tools such as Poll Everywhere or Kahoot! can be used for this purpose. If you plan to use polling during the semester, you can use this activity as a way to orient students to the polling tool and get them familiar with the syllabus. Students report higher levels of engagement and learning when polling tools are used. This was demonstrated in a study conducted by Wang (2015) where 90% of students in the study indicated being engaged and motivated when using Kahoot! and approximately 75% of the students indicated that the Kahoot! quizzes helped them learn the content. See Figure 7.1 for a sample open-ended syllabus quiz and Figure 7.2 for a sample multiple-choice and true–false syllabus quiz.

Figure 7.1. Sample open-ended syllabus quiz.

1. What will you be able to know, think, or do as a result of participating in this class?

2. How does this course fit into your overall program or major requirements?

3. What are the major topics that will be addressed in the course?

4. What textbook or other readings are required?

5. What is the best way to reach me?

6. What campus resources are available to you if you need help?

7. What are the major assignments, and what is the value of these assignments?

8. What is the average weekly workload?

9. What do you need to do before, during, and after class?

10. Why does academic integrity matter, and what are the policies about honest and dishonest behaviors?

11. Will you be able to make up an exam or submit work late if needed?

12. Are there extra credit opportunities?

13. How many quizzes and exams will there be?

14. Where can you find information on assignment expectations?

15. How will your final grade in the course be determined?

Figure 7.2. Sample multiple-choice and true–false syllabus quiz.

1. What is the best way to reach me?
   a. E-mail
   b. Phone
   c. Text
2. When is your first assignment due?
   a. September 10th
   b. September 15th
   c. October 1st
3. Late work will be accepted.
   a. True
   b. False
4. Extra credit is available.
   a. True
   b. False
5. What page of the syllabus contains information on the academic integrity policy?
   a. 1
   b. 3
   c. 8
6. How much does the final exam count toward your final grade?
   a. 15%
   b. 20%
   c. 30%
7. What is the minimum grade needed for an A in the course?
   a. 90
   b. 92
   c. 94
8. Assignment rubrics are included in the syllabus.
   a. True
   b. False
9. How many exams will there be?
   a. 1
   b. 2
   c. 4
10. How many learning outcomes are there?
    a. 2
    b. 4
    c. 5

News Clip Course Introduction

An alternative approach to a syllabus icebreaker is the news clip course introduction. For this activity, small groups of three to four students review the syllabus and work together to create a one- to two-minute overview of the course that would be appropriate for a brief news report on a morning television show. Groups can then share their news reports with the class. The sharing could happen live during class or could be recorded and uploaded into the course learning management system. The benefit of this activity is that the limited amount of time for the news video encourages students to focus or zoom in on what is most important.

Round-Robin Activity

Claudia Lilie (personal communication, March 2017) suggested using a round-robin activity where students review the syllabus on the first day to answer questions posted around the room on large sticky notes. Place students in small groups, with one marker color for each group, and have them rotate around the room. They must come to consensus on the answer and write it down. Once they rotate to a new station, they can write down their answer or edit an answer already written down. If they totally agree with what is written, they will place a check mark by that response. When time is up, they will stay standing by their last sticky note and have to defend their answer. The concluding activity is to have them summarize the five most important bullets from the charts. This helps you hear what the students find most important about the course and allows you to expand on areas that were missed.

Negotiation and Collaboration Exercise

A negotiation and collaboration exercise can be used on the first day to orient students to the syllabus (Kaplan & Renard, 2015). To engage students in this activity, you need to decide which parts of your syllabus are negotiable. The specific components of the syllabus are then shared with the students in your class. For example, you may be willing to negotiate due dates, weighting of assignments (usually within a range), or even policies. Kaplan and Renard (2015) recommended presenting negotiable items in extreme terms such as a zero-tolerance policy, because this makes it easier for students to get started with the negotiation process. Students are placed in teams of four to six students, and these teams will negotiate with you to determine the final syllabus for the course. Although this approach can work well in many different classes, it may be particularly useful in business courses where negotiation skills are learned, because it will give students the opportunity to practice these skills and make connections between personal experiences and course concepts.

Brainwriting

Brainwriting exercises on the syllabus and course can be used on the first day of class. Brainwriting involves asking students to write down ideas before engaging in group discussion (Heslin, 2009). The following are the steps involved with brainwriting:

- Students are typically assigned to small groups of approximately four to six students. Groups are then given a prompt to write about. In this case, students could be asked to write down one important idea from the syllabus on an index card.
- After writing down one idea, students pass the index card to the person on their right. At this point, each student should have an index card with one idea written on it.
- Now students have to write down another important piece of information from the syllabus, but the catch is that students cannot write any idea they already wrote down or read on the index card. As you can imagine, this task becomes more challenging with time.
- This process is repeated until each index card is returned to the person who wrote down the first idea on the card.
- Students then discuss the important elements in their group.

Researchers have found that having this time to think and engage in brainwriting leads to more productive group conversations (Heslin, 2009; Paulus, 2000; Paulus & Yang, 2000). As you can imagine, having time to think prior to discussing can be helpful. This approach also ensures that the opinions and ideas of all members are shared with the group.

Reciprocal Interview

The reciprocal interview is another activity for the first day of class that not only focuses on the course and syllabus but also helps students get to know one another. According to Foster and Hermann (2011), the reciprocal interview involves the following steps:

- Groups of 5 or 6 students are formed. Groups are given approximately 10 to 15 minutes to review the syllabus and discuss course expectations, using questions posed by the instructor. For example, the instructor could ask students what are the learning outcomes, how will the instructor evaluate learning, and what does the instructor expect of students (Foster & Hermann, 2011). This discussion serves as preparation for an interview by the instructor.
- Each group identifies a member who will serve as the representative of the group during the interview phase.

- The instructor then asks the representative from each group a series of questions about the syllabus and course expectations. During this process, the instructor mostly listens but can provide clarification as needed.
- Each group now selects a new representative and has 5 to 10 minutes to develop questions to ask the instructor.
- The newly selected representatives interview the instructor, asking the questions they just developed. After answering the questions posed by the groups, the instructor can then highlight a few important course-related issues that were not yet addressed.

Foster and Hermann (2011) found that students who participated in the reciprocal interview reported at the end of the semester higher levels of comfort approaching the instructor and higher levels of comfort participating in class. In a related study, students who participated in the reciprocal interview on the first day reported that the overall course experience was more valuable than students who did not participate in an icebreaker activity (Hermann, Foster, & Hardin, 2010).

Jigsaw Classroom Syllabus Activity

One of the most effective strategies for group work is the Jigsaw Classroom Exercise. This approach can be used to get students familiar with the syllabus on the first day of class. The Jigsaw Classroom Exercise (Aronson et al., 1978) involves having students work in a group to develop expertise on a topic so that they are able to teach their group members about the topic. Often, pre-work is involved so that students come into the learning environment with some background knowledge, but this is not always necessary. In the case of the Jigsaw Classroom Syllabus Activity, pre-work would not be necessary. Here's how it works.

Students are placed in what are called *home base groups*. Groups of four students are formed. To save time, you can walk around the room and identify clusters of four students who are sitting near one another. Each group must have at least four members, so if there is a group that has three or fewer members, students should be assigned to another group so that a few groups have five members.

After students are assigned to their home base group, each member of each group will need to be assigned to different pages of the syllabus (e.g., pages 1–3, pages 4–6, pages 7–10). In other words, every member of the home base group should be assigned a different section of the syllabus. If a group has more than four members, then two students will have to share a section of the syllabus. You can either assign students their section by handing out index cards with the pages associated with each section, or you can simply ask students to decide among themselves who will focus on which sections. This part of the process should not take more than a couple of minutes.

Next, you will ask all of the students assigned to each section to move to different parts of the room. For example, you could say if you are focusing on pages 1–3, come to the front right corner of the room, if you are focusing on pages 4–6, come to the front left corner of the room, and so forth. Students will need to take their syllabus and notebook with them to their assigned location.

These newly formed groups are called *expert groups*, because the students in each group are focusing on different content and need to learn the content well enough so that they can teach the material to their home base group members later on. While in this expert group, students will review their assigned section of the syllabus, identifying the most important information that they would like to bring to the attention of their home base group members. As expert group members discuss their assigned pages of the syllabus, they can reach out to you with questions. During this part of the process, it is important for you to check in with all groups to confirm that they have a strong understanding of the syllabus and that their focus is on target. One effective way to check in with groups is to ask group members, "What are the key points you plan to emphasize, and why?" This approach works much better than asking, "How's it going? Any questions?" because the latter approach doesn't assist you in confirming that the group members are mastering the content. If students do not fully understand the content, it is possible that they will be teaching their home base group members incorrect information. Thus, your role in confirming that students are on track during this part of the activity is essential. This part of the activity takes the most time.

After students have had the opportunity to master the syllabus content in their assigned section, they return to their home base group. At this point, you can give each student approximately 2 minutes to teach his or her group members about the important content contained in the assigned section of the syllabus. You can time this to ensure that all students get an equal amount of time. At the conclusion of 2 minutes, you can make an announcement to inform students that they need to switch to the student who learned about the next section. Repeat this process until all students have had the opportunity to teach their fellow group members their assigned content. You can then give the group an additional 2 minutes to ask clarifying questions and fill in any information gaps. Because there are 4 sections being used and 1 summary opportunity, this part of the process should take a total of 10 minutes.

The final step of this activity is to have a brief large group discussion, providing answers to questions posed by students or adding emphasis to a part of the syllabus that needs more attention. For the Jigsaw Classroom Syllabus Activity, approximately 10 to 20 minutes will typically be needed.

There are many benefits to the Jigsaw Classroom Syllabus Activity. For one, Walker and Crogan (1998) found that students who participate in Jigsaw Classroom Exercises have improved academic performance, developed better attitudes toward their peers, and reduced levels of prejudice. These benefits are probably in part due to the fact that this group activity requires students to work with other students who may be different from them in many ways. Another benefit of using this approach is that all students are accountable. Because each member of the group is responsible for different content, one person in the group can't carry the weight of the group and do all the work; all members of the group must be actively involved so that they can teach their fellow home base group members. The Jigsaw Classroom Exercise is a terrific technique to eliminate or greatly reduce social loafing in group work, and this early introduction to this active learning approach can make it easier to replicate in future class meetings. After participating in the Jigsaw Classroom Syllabus Activity, students will know how this activity works and will be able to quickly move from the home base group to the expert group and back to the home base group with ease in the future when you use this approach with course-related content. Students are more likely to function productively in a group when they receive training and support on how to best function in a group setting (Prichard, Stratford, & Bizo, 2006). The structured nature of the Jigsaw Classroom Exercise provides students with a model for engaging in group work in and outside of class. The Jigsaw Classroom Syllabus Activity is a great way to familiarize students with the syllabus, make connections to several other classmates, and develop essential soft skills such as teamwork and communication that will serve students well in college and their career, as these skills are highly desired by employers (Costigan & Donahue, 2009; Koc, 2011).

SYLLABUS ACTIVITIES THROUGHOUT THE SEMESTER

It is easy to leave the syllabus there, at the beginning of the semester shortly after the document has been presented and/or discussed. But there are many ways to continue to emphasize the importance of the syllabus throughout the semester, helping students use the syllabus as a course resource, much like their textbook. As faculty, we can model and encourage using the syllabus on a regular basis. For starters, inform your students that they will need to bring their syllabus to every class (either electronically or on paper).

Consider using a mini syllabus review at the start of every class, once every week, or at the start of a new unit or module. During a mini syllabus review, you can ask students to work with a partner to review the syllabus to identify the learning objectives and focus of the day or week and to determine what upcoming activities and assignments need their attention. After giving students a couple of minutes for this purpose, you can randomly call on students or ask for student volunteers to share the learning outcomes and important upcoming assignments or activities and answer any questions they might have.

Encouraging students to review assignment expectations is another great way to use the syllabus as a resource throughout the semester. For example, you could direct your students' attention to assignment details when reminding them about an upcoming assignment. An example early in the semester could be the reading assignment, especially if you have included guided reading questions. For an example of how reading assignment questions are shared with students via the syllabus, see the "Reading Assignments/Final Exam Review Sheet" section of the sample syllabus on page 175 in the Appendix. For a more active approach, have students independently review the assignment details in the syllabus a few weeks before the due date, including rubrics if provided, and then do a quick "turn and talk" with a classmate about the assignment. During the turn and talk, students can share their understanding of the assignment, identify questions or areas needing clarification, and identify resources such as the library that might be helpful when completing the assignment. This process is most useful when you have embedded important assignment information into the syllabus. For several examples of assignment details, see the "Assignment Details and Grading Rubrics" section in the sample syllabus (see the Appendix, pages 165–176). After the turn and talk activity, you can shift to a large group discussion to address questions so all students can benefit from hearing your responses to the questions. This activity does not need to take very much class time; often just five minutes will suffice. In addition to reminding students of the valuable content contained in the syllabus and helping students use the syllabus as a resource, this brief activity will also reduce the number of questions you get from students about the assignment via e-mail throughout the week. More important, it can also increase the likelihood that the products submitted match your expectations.

Another opportunity is presented when a daily exit question is asked. At the end of every class, you could ask your students the following two questions:

1. What is the most important thing you learned today?
2. What questions do you still have that remain unanswered?

If several students ask questions about something that is addressed within the syllabus, you can remind them about the value of the syllabus and encourage them to dive back into the syllabus to find the answer. This allows students to find the answers on their own and shows them that the syllabus is a valuable resource.

A reflective exercise at mid-semester is another great strategy that can bring students' attention back to the syllabus. A mid-semester reflection exercise involves asking students to take out their syllabus to review the learning outcomes for the course and assess their progress toward these learning outcomes. Remind students that the course is approximately halfway complete, so achievement of learning outcomes is not expected at this time; however, it is important for students to determine if they are on track to meet these goals by the end of the semester. During this reflective process, it can also be very helpful for students to review the workload, noting what they have already completed and what still needs to be done. Developing an action plan to complete upcoming tasks can be helpful and can be included in the reflection. This is also a good time for students to consider their grade in the course thus far. Students may find it helpful to document their grades on assignments on the syllabus itself, especially if the syllabus clearly conveys how much each assignment counts toward the final grade. This reflective process can be repeated again at the end of the semester. Engaging students in reflective practices while using the syllabus as a resource will help them develop skills that will serve them well in the future.

CHAPTER SUMMARY

When the syllabus becomes a living, breathing document that is used often throughout the course of a semester, it becomes a valuable teaching and learning tool for both the faculty and the students. How you breathe life into it depends on your course goals and objectives. However, finding ways to actively engage students with the syllabus from day one will help them realize the value of this important document. With continued effort and reflective practice, you will help your students navigate your course and their own learning with more ease.

REFERENCES

Anderson, D. M., McGuire, F. A., & Cory, L. (2011). The first day: It happens only once. *Teaching in Higher Education, 16*(3), 293–303.

Aronson, E., Blaney, N., Stephan, C., Sikes, J., & Snapp, M. (1978). *The jigsaw class-room.* Beverley Hills, CA: Sage.

Bassett, J. F., & Nix, P. M. (2011). Students' first day of class preferences: Factor structure and individual differences. *North American Journal of Psychology, 13*(3), 373–382.

Buchert, S., Laws, E. L., Apperson, J. M., & Bregman, N. J. (2008). First impressions and professor reputation: Influence on student evaluations of instruction. *Social Psychology of Education, 11*(4), 397–408. doi:10.1007/s11218-008-9055-1

Costigan, R. D., & Donahue, L. (2009). Developing the great eight competencies with leaderless group discussion. *Journal of Management Education, 33*(5), 596–616.

Creasey, G., Jarvis, P., & Knapnik, E. (2009). A measure to assess student–instructor relationships. *International Journal for the Scholarship of Teaching, 3*(2). Retrieved from https://doi.org/10.20429/ijsotl.2009.030214

Dixon, J. S., Crooks, H., & Henry, K. (2006). Breaking the ice: Supporting collaboration and the development of community online. *Canadian Journal of Learning and Technology, 32*(2), 1–20.

Eggleston, T., & Smith, G. (2004). Building community in the classroom through icebreakers and parting ways. Society for the Teaching of Psychology Office of Teaching Resources in Psychology. Retrieved from http://teachpsych.org/resources/Documents/otrp/resources/eggleston04.pdf

Fornaciari, C. J., & Dean, K. L. (2014). The 21st-century syllabus: From pedagogy to andragogy. *Journal of Management Education, 38*(5), 701–723. doi:10.1177/1052562913504763

Foster, D. A., & Hermann, A. D. (2011). Linking the first of class to end-of-term satisfaction: Using a reciprocal interview activity to create an active and comfortable classroom. *College Teaching, 59*(3), 111–116.

Gannon, K. (2016, August). The absolute worst way to start the semester. *Chronicle Vitae.* Retrieved from https://chroniclevitae.com/news/1498-the-absolute-worst-way-to-start-the-semester

Glascoff, D. W. (1984). The syllabus quiz: A multipurpose strategy. *Journal of Marketing Education, 6*(3), 46–49.

Guertin, L. (2014, August). Getting students to read the syllabus with a syllabus quiz. American Geophysical Union Blogosphere. Retrieved from http://blogs.agu.org/geoedtrek/2014/08/27/syllabus-quiz/

Harrington, C., & Gabert-Quillen, C. (2015). Syllabus length and use of images: An empirical investigation of student perceptions. *Scholarship of Teaching and Learning in Psychology, 1*(3), 235–243.

Harton, H. C., Richardson, D. S., Barreras, R. E., Rockloff, M. J., & Latane, B. (2002). Focused interactive learning: A tool for active class discussion. *Teaching of Psychology, 29*(1), 10–15.

Hermann, A. D., Foster, D. A., & Hardin, E. E. (2010). Does the first week of class matter? A quasi-experimental investigation of student satisfaction. *Teaching of Psychology, 37,* 79–84.

Heslin, P. A. (2009). Better than brainstorming? Potential contextual boundary conditions to brainwriting for idea generation in organizations. *Journal of Occupational and Organizational Psychology, 82*(1), 129–145. doi:10.1348/096317908X285642

Kamin, C., Glicken, A., Hall, M., Quarantillo, B., & Merenstein, G. (2001). Evaluation of electronic discussion groups as a teaching/learning strategy in an evidence-based medicine course: A pilot study. *Education for Health, 14*(1), 21–32. doi:10.1080/1357628001001538 0

Kaplan, D. M., & Renard, M. K. (2015). Negotiating your syllabus: Building a collaborative contract. *Journal of Management Education, 39*(3), 400–421. doi:10.1177/1052562914565788

Kim, A. N., & Shakory, S. (2017). Early, but not intermediate, evaluative feedback predicts cumulative exam scores in large lecture-style post-secondary education classrooms. *Scholarship of Teaching and Learning in Psychology, 3*(2), 141–150. doi:10.1037/stl0000086

Koc, E. W. (2011). Getting noticed, getting hired: Candidate attributes that recruiters seek. *NACE Journal, 72*(2), 14–19.

Laws, E. L., Apperson, J. M., Buchert, S., & Bregman, N. J. (2010). Student evaluations of instruction: When are enduring first impressions formed? *North American Journal of Psychology, 12*(1), 81–92.

Legg, A. M., & Wilson, J. H. (2009). E-mail from professor enhances student motivation and attitudes. *Teaching of Psychology, 36*(3), 205–211. doi:10.1080/00986280902960034

McDaniel, M. A., Wildman, K. M., & Anderson, J. L. (2012). Using quizzes to enhance summative-assessment performance in a web-based class: An experimental study. *Journal of Applied Research in Memory and Cognition, 1*(1), 18–26. doi:10.1016/j.jarmac.2011.10.001

McGinley, J. J., & Jones, B. D. (2014). A brief instructional intervention to increase students' motivation on the first day of class. *Teaching of Psychology, 41*(2), 158–162.

Parish, T. S., & Campbell, N. J. (1977). Consistency of students' evaluations of instructors. *Journal of Instructional Psychology, 4*(2), 30–33.

Paulus, P. B. (2000). Groups, teams, and creativity: The creative potential of idea generating groups. *Applied Psychology: An International Review, 49*(2), 237–262. doi:10.1111/1464-0597.00013

Paulus, P. B., & Yang, H. (2000). Idea generation in groups: A basis for creativity in organizations. *Organizational Behavior and Human Decision Processes*, 82(1), 76–87.

Prichard, J. S., Stratford, R. J., & Bizo, L. A. (2006). Team-skills training enhances collaborative learning. *Learning and Instruction*, 16(3), 256–265. doi:10.1016/j.learninstruc.2006.03.005

Raymark, P. H., & Connor-Greene, P. A. (2002). The syllabus quiz. *The Teaching of Psychology*, 29(4), 286–288.

Roediger, H., & Karpicke, J. D. (2006). Test-enhanced learning: Taking memory tests improves long-term retention. *Psychological Science*, 17(3), 249–255. doi:10.1111/j.1467-9280.2006.01693.x

Rovai, A. P. (2002). Building sense of community at a distance. *International Review of Research in Open and Distance Learning*, 3(1). Retrieved from http://www.irrodl.org/index.php/irrodl/article/viewArticle/79/152

Slusser, S. R., & Erickson, R. J. (2006). Group quizzes: An extension of the collaborative learning process. *Teaching Sociology*, 34(1), 249–262.

Smith, M. F., & Razzouk, N. Y. (1993). Improving classroom communication: The case of the course syllabus. *Journal of Education for Business*, 68(4), 215–222.

Stratton, G. (2011). Does increasing textbook portability increase reading rates or academic performance? *Inquiry*, 16(1), 5–16.

Taras, M. (2006). Do unto others or not: Equity in feedback for undergraduates. *Assessment and Evaluation in Higher Education*, 31(3), 365–377.

Thompson, B. (2007). The syllabus as a communication document: Constructing and presenting the syllabus. *Communication Education*, 56(1), 54–71. doi:10.1080/03634520601011575

Walker, I., & Crogan, M. (1998). Academic performance, prejudice, and the jigsaw classroom: New pieces to the puzzle. *Journal of Community and Applied Social Psychology*, 8(6), 381–393.

Wang, A. I. (2015). The wear out effect of a game-based student response system. *Computers and Education*, 82, 217–227. doi:10.1016/j.compedu.2014.11.004

Weimer, M. (2013, August). Five things to do on the first day of class. *The Teaching Professor Blog*. Faculty Focus: Higher Ed Teaching Strategies from Magna Publication. Retrieved from https://www.facultyfocus.com/articles/teaching-professor-blog/five-things-to-do-on-the-first-day-of-class/

APPENDIX

SAMPLE SYLLABUS

Welcome to
Educational Psychology!

PSY 226-02

Meets on Tuesdays 9:30 a.m.–12:20 p.m. BH 203

Note. Photo by Tom Peterson. Reprinted with permission.

Professor Contact Information: Please reach out to me!

Dr. Christine Harrington
charrington@middlesexcc.edu; 732.548.6000
Office Location: Center I

Office Hours: Mondays 9:00 a.m.–11:00 a.m. and 3:30 p.m.–4:30 p.m.
Thursdays 1:00 p.m.–2:00 p.m. and 3:30 p.m.–4:30 p.m.

What Is This Course All About?

Prerequisites: PSY 123

This course provides an overview of learning, motivational, and developmental theories with a focus on their application to the field of education. Educational research addressing the powerful role of the educator, effective teaching strategies, and curriculum decision-making are discussed. Theory- and research-based practices to reach all learners in an educational environment are emphasized.

Learning Outcomes (LOs)

Here's what you will be able to do after successfully completing this course:

1. Identify and discuss learning, motivational, and developmental theories and psychological concepts related to education. (Bloom's taxonomy: remembering and understanding) LO1
2. Describe the various educational research methods and apply this knowledge to evaluate educational research studies. (Bloom's taxonomy: understanding, applying, evaluating) LO2
3. Determine best classroom and institutional practices in education. (Bloom's taxonomy: applying, analyzing, evaluating) LO3
4. Integrate theory and research to develop and implement a lesson plan related to educational psychology. (Bloom's taxonomy: creating) LO4

As you can imagine, these are important skills you will need as a future educator. The knowledge and skills gained in this course will help you meet with success in future courses, such as the Educational Field Experience. For example, the lesson planning experience you gain in this course will help you write more effective lesson plans in your practicum courses. As you know, this course is just one of the many educational courses you'll need to take to graduate. This course will help you develop a strong foundational knowledge in theories, research, and educational concepts so that you can apply this knowledge in a variety of educational situations and settings.

Course Content Areas

Educator and Educational Setting	Theories	Research-Based Practices in Teaching and Assessment
Connection between the role of the educator and student motivation and learning; current trends and contemporary issues; classroom environment; school climate; diversity and culture; home–school connections	Cognitive, social-emotional, language development theories; learning theory (operant conditioning, observational learning, memory process, problem-solving, constructivism); motivational theories (behavioral, cognitive, humanistic, social)	Review of research methods; classroom management, teaching methods (direct instruction, cooperative learning, differentiated instruction); objective driven lesson planning (Bloom's taxonomy); evaluating and grading learning through assessment; high-stakes testing; teaching with technology

Teaching Philosophy

I am incredibly honored to have the opportunity to be a part of your learning journey. I believe that the magic of learning takes place through powerful student–professor relationships, strong peer–peer relationships, and engaging learning tasks. As a result, I want to get to know you in and outside of the classroom, and I want to help you develop strong connections with your peers. I have carefully planned the learning activities so that we are focused on content and skills that really matter in the field of education. You can expect that I will bring a high level of enthusiasm and energy to the classroom every day and that you will be both challenged and supported throughout this learning experience.

Some information about me: I earned my BA in psychology and my MA in counseling and personnel services from the College of New Jersey, and my PhD in counseling psychology from Lehigh University. I've been working in higher education for almost 20 years, first as a counselor and disability services provider and then as a full-time faculty member. I also served as the director of the Center for Learning and Teaching. Currently, I am serving a 2-year term as the executive director of the Center for Student Success at the New Jersey Council of County Colleges. I'm the author of 2 books: *Student Success in College: Doing What Works!* (3rd edition) and *Dynamic Lecturing: Research-Based Strategies to Enhance Lecture Effectiveness* (2017). I've also been serving on the board of education in my hometown school district for almost 10 years. On a personal note, I am married and have 2 teenage boys. All of these professional and personal experiences inform my teaching.

What Can I Expect to Happen During Class?

In order to learn, you'll need to be actively involved and engaged with the course content, so you can expect this semester to be filled with lively discussions, activities, and challenging assignments. Because we learn best when engaged with others, you will work with a partner or small group almost every class period and I'll be there to support you!

Note. Photo by Tom Peterson. Reprinted with permission.

What Book and Other Materials Do I Need?

Textbook: *Educational Psychology* (12th edition) by Anita Woolfolk
Research Article Packet: This will be distributed in class.

Available Help and Support

Successful people access support from others as needed. Middlesex County College has many supportive services that can help you as you strive to achieve your goals. I encourage you to reach out to me or other professionals on campus. Here's some information about the resources available to you.

Your Professor	E-mail me at charrington@middlesexcc.edu or stop by my office.
Librarians	The library offers assistance with finding and evaluating information. Visit the library, call 732.548.6000, or visit the website for online options.
Counselors	The Counseling and Career Services department offers confidential individual counseling. Visit Edison Hall Room 100, call 732.548.6000, or visit the website for more information.
Tutors	The tutoring center, located in JLC 240, offers tutoring support in many subjects. Call 732.548.6000 or see the website for details.
Academic Advisers	The Academic Advising Center offers drop-in advising services. Visit CH 109, call 732.548.6000, or visit the website.

The Best Way to Study/Learn (According to Research!)

Studying is an important part of college, right? McGuire (2015) actually recommends that you shift your focus from studying to learning. Even though using the right study techniques may get you a good grade on a test, engaging in powerful learning strategies will help you really understand the content so you can use this knowledge now and in the future. By using the following strategies, you will not only make better use of your time but also discover that your learning really increases and stays with you over the long term (and a bonus is that you'll do well on your exams too!).

1. **Build Background Knowledge Before Reading:** Review the table of contents and chapter summary or Google the topic before reading the textbook chapters. For peer-reviewed research, read the abstract several times, then the introduction and discussion sections before reading the entire article. Building your background knowledge will increase the likelihood that you will comprehend the readings (Recht & Leslie, 1998).

2. **Actively Read:** Use the 3R approach. Read: Start with a small section. Recite: Close the book and take notes. Review: Go back and reread this section, filling in notes, and highlighting if you'd like, limiting your highlighting to one to two sentences per paragraph (McDaniel, Howard, & Einstein, 2009).

3. **Mentally Organize, Visualize, and Apply Content:** Think about how concepts are connected to each other, identify examples, use visual images, and put content into your own words (Dickinson & O'Connell, 1990; Gadzella & Baloglu, 2003).

4. **Repackage Your Notes:** Combine your reading and discussion board notes using a visually effective organizational note-taking approach such as tables (the matrix approach) or concept maps (Kiewra et al., 1991).

5. **Test Yourself Often:** Use the practice questions available online or create your own questions or flashcards with a tool such as Quizlet. Testing has been found to be one of the best ways to learn (Roediger & Karpicke, 2006).

6. **Study Together and Teach:** Students who study together outperform students who study alone. Teaching is an incredibly powerful way to learn, so find a study group member, family member, or friend who wants to learn about psychology and teach them (Schwartz, Son, Kornell, & Finn, 2011)!

7. **Seek Help:** Discover the many resources available to you, and take advantage of these resources. Students who reach out for help do better (Strage et al., 2002)!

Your Learning Experience

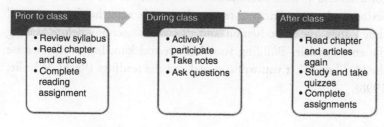

Important Policy Information

Middlesex County College welcomes all students with disabilities.
If you need accommodations because of a disability, contact Disability Services in
Edison Hall Room 100, 732.906.2546.

To foster a productive learning environment, the college requires that all students
adhere to the Code of Student Conduct, which is published in the college catalog and
on the website.

Participation Policy

You are expected to be an active participant in class discussions and other learning opportunities. To do this, you must be prepared, so be sure to complete all reading and other assignments according to the schedule. The class activities have been carefully designed to help you achieve the learning outcomes for the course. Missing class or not actively participating will negatively affect your ability to learn the content.

Academic Integrity Policy:
All Students Are Expected to Engage in Academically Honest Work

Academic integrity benefits everyone in our community. It not only helps you reach the real goal of this class—learning—but also allows for the college and program to be perceived positively by others. When students are dishonest, they lose out on valuable learning that will help them perform well in their career. It can also negatively affect all of the students in the program and at the institution by creating negative mind-sets that may result in fewer outside learning opportunities for students. Academic dishonesty is any attempt by a student to gain academic advantage through dishonest means or to assist another student with gaining an unfair advantage. Academic integrity is important regardless of whether the work is graded or ungraded, group or individual, written or oral. Dishonest acts can result in a failing grade on an assignment, a failing course grade, and/or an official code of conduct charge being filed.

Late Work/Missed Exam Policy:
All Students Are Expected to Complete Learning Tasks on Schedule

It is important to stay on track with your assignments; not only will this help you feel less stressed, but it is also an important skill you will need in your career. Being able to meet deadlines and juggle many tasks are important career and life skills. Thus, you will need to complete all quizzes, exams, and assignments according to the schedule. However, I recognize that personal circumstances may at times make it difficult or impossible to complete a learning task on schedule. If you have a personal situation that prevents you from completing a task on time, you will need to discuss this with me prior to the due date if possible, or as soon as it becomes possible, so that we can come up with a plan. Reading assignments can be submitted PRIOR to class in the learning management system if you will be absent. Extensions are at my discretion. If an extension is provided, it is important to know that the format of the exam or the assignment may be modified.

Registrar Withdrawal Information

Students sometimes have a need to withdraw from a class because of personal or academic reasons. Click here for deadline dates. If you do encounter difficulties, please contact me prior to withdrawing.

Course Outline

Week	What Is Due?	Topic of the Day
9/2		*Learning Objectives: You will be able to:* 1. *Discuss how teacher and student behaviors influence the learning process. (LO1)* 2. *Describe research methods to assess educational practices. (LO2)* **Chapter 1: Learning, Teaching, and Educational Psychology** What Is Educational Psychology? Teachers and Students Research in Education Academic Integrity Brooks: Mind-set of a Teacher
9/9	Academic Integrity Quiz Chapter 1 Quiz Reading Assignment Chapters 1 and 14	*Learning Objectives: You will be able to:* 1. *Describe the characteristics of effective teachers. (LO1)* 2. *Write learning outcomes according to Bloom's taxonomy. (LO4)* 3. *Develop a lesson plan. (LO4)* 4. *Describe practices associated with differentiated instruction. (LO3)* **Chapter 14: Teaching Every Student** *Hogan, Rabinowitz, and Kraven (2003); Krathwohl and Anderson (2010)* Effective Teachers Lesson Plans and Bloom's Taxonomy Teaching Strategies and Teacher Expectations Differentiated Instruction GROUP ASSIGNMENTS FOR LITERATURE REVIEW PRESENTATION
9/16	Chapter 14 Quiz Reading Assignment Chapter 15	*Learning Objectives: You will be able to:* 1. *Determine assessment methods aligned to learning outcomes. (LO3)* 2. *Explain the pros and cons of rubrics. (LO3)* 3. *Discuss the pros and cons of standardized testing. (LO3)* **Chapter 15: Classroom Assessment, Grading, and Standardized Testing** *Zimmerman and DiBenedetto (2008)* Test and Measurements Assessment Options Grading and Rubrics Standardized Testing

(Continues)

Week	What Is Due?	Topic of the Day
9/23	Chapter 15 Quiz Reading Assignment Chapter 2 **Literature Review Paper Due**	*Learning Objectives: You will be able to:* 1. **Discuss the importance of considering developmental factors when developing a lesson plan. (LO1; LO4)** 2. **Compare and contrast Piaget and Vygotsky's theories. (LO1)** **Chapter 2: Cognitive Development** *Goswami (2008); Mayer (2009)* Neurons and Brain Development Piaget and Vygotsky GROUP WORK
9/30	Chapter 2 Quiz Reading Assignment Chapters 3 and 4	*Learning Objectives: You will be able to:* 1. **Identify teacher actions that can decrease academic dishonesty. (LO3)** 2. **Summarize special education laws. (LO1)** 3. **Describe learning disabilities and ADHD. (LO1)** 4. **Articulate strategies to reduce learned helplessness. (LO1)** **Chapter 3: The Self, Social, and Moral Development** Bronfenbrenner, Peer Issues, and Bullying Erikson and Kohlberg Cheating **Chapter 4: Learner Differences and Learning Needs** Intelligence and the Bell Curve Learning Styles Special Education Law Learning Disabilities and ADHD Seligman's Learned Helplessness Gifted Students GROUP WORK
10/7	Chapters 3 and 4 Quizzes **Lesson Plan 1 and Power Point Slides Due (Learning Outcomes; Outline of Content)**	*Learning Objectives: You will be able to:* 1. **Develop a lesson plan and related visual presentation. (LO4)** **Chapters 3 and 4 Continued** *Ramstetter, Murray, and Garner (2010)* *National Reading Panel (2000)* GROUP WORK

Week	What Is Due?	Topic of the Day
10/14	Prepare for Midterm!	*Learning Objectives: You will be able to:* *1. Demonstrate knowledge of major educational psychology concepts. (LO1)* **Midterm** (Chapters 14, 15, 1, 2, 3, 4) GROUP WORK
10/21	Prepare Presentation	*Learning Objectives: You will be able to:* *1. Work collaboratively with peers to create and deliver a presentation on a research article related to Educational Psychology. (LO2)* **Literature Review Presentations** GROUP ASSIGNMENTS FOR 30-MINUTE PRESENTATION
10/28	Reading Assignment Chapters 5 and 6 **Lesson Plan 2 Due**	*Learning Objectives: You will be able to:* *1. Describe bilingual programs. (LO3)* *2. Discuss how culture and diversity play a role in learning. (LO1)* **Chapter 5: Language Development, Language Diversity, and Immigrant Education** Language Milestones Bilingualism **Chapter 6: Culture and Diversity** Culture, Social Class, and Gender Tracking Resilience
11/4	Chapters 5 and 6 Quizzes Reading Assignment Chapter 7 and 13 **Reflection Paper 1 Due**	*Learning Objectives: You will be able to:* *1. Identify behavioral management strategies. (LO1)* *2. Evaluate the effectiveness of various behavioral management strategies. (LO3)* **Chapter 7: Behavioral Views of Learning** Classical and Operant Conditioning Observational Learning **Chapter 13: Creating Learning Environments** First Day of Class Classroom Management Teacher Effectiveness Physical Environment GROUP WORK

(Continues)

Week	What Is Due?	Topic of the Day
11/11		**College Closed: Veterans Day**
11/18	Reading Assignment Chapters 8 and 9 Chapters 7 and 13 Quizzes	*Learning Objectives: You will be able to:* 1. *Describe the memory process. (LO1)* 2. *Identify teaching strategies that facilitate the development of metacognition and critical thinking. (LO1)* **Chapter 8: Cognitive Views of Learning** Acquiring Knowledge, Attention and Memory Forgetting **Chapter 9: Complex Cognitive Processes** Metacognition Note-Taking Creative and Critical Thinking **APA Task Force on Zero Tolerance Policies (2008) Student Presentation** **Recht and Leslie (1998) Prior Knowledge Student Presentation**
11/25	Chapters 8 and 9 Quizzes Reading Assignment Chapters 10, 11, and 12	*Learning Objectives: You will be able to:* 1. *Describe constructivism. (LO1)* 2. *Compare and contrast various motivational theories. (LO1, LO3)* **Chapter 10: The Learning Sciences and Constructivism** What Is Constructivism? John Dewey Cooperative Group Work Technology and Instruction **Chapter 11: Social Cognitive Views of Learning and Motivation** Bandura Self-Efficacy Self-Regulated Learning **Chapter 12: Motivation in Learning and Teaching** Motivational Approaches/Theories Intrinsic and Extrinsic Motivation Maslow Attribution Theory Emotions **Memory Student Presentation (Schwartz, Son, Kornell, & Finn, 2011)** **Fully Guided Instruction Student Presentation (Clark, Kircshner, and Sweller 2012)**

Week	What Is Due?	Topic of the Day
12/2	Chapters 10, 11, and 12 Quizzes	*Learning Objectives: You will be able to:* 1. *Develop a presentation on motivational strategies. (LO1, LO2)* 2. *Engage in self-regulation processes to determine readiness for the final exam. (LO1)* **Chapters 10–12 Continued** *Motivation Student Presentation (Wlodkowski, 1999)* *Final Exam Review*
12/9	Prepare for Final Exam **Reflection Paper 2 Due**	*Learning Objectives: You will be able to:* 1. *Demonstrate knowledge and skills learned via the final exam. (LO1, LO2, LO3)* *Final Exam*

Grading Information

Lesson Plans (LO4)	5%	Research Article Presentation (LO2, LO4)	10%
Reflection Papers (LO1)	5%	Literature Review Presentation (LO2, LO4)	15%
Reading Assignments (LO1)	10%	Midterm (LO1, LO2, LO3)	15%
Quizzes (LO1, LO2, LO3)	10%	Final Exam (LO1, LO2, LO3)	20%
Literature Review Paper (LO2)	10%		

Grading Scheme

A	A–	B+	B	B–
(93–100)	(90–92.9)	(87–89.9)	(83–86.9)	(80–82.9)

C+	C	D	F (64.4 or below)
(77–79.9)	(70–76.9)	(65–69.9)	

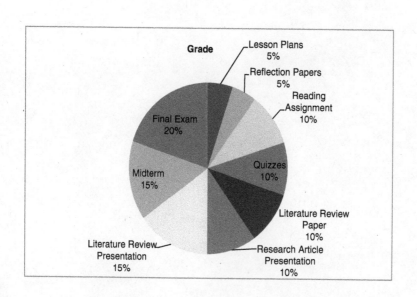

Assignment Details and Grading Rubrics

Lesson Plans

Learning to write lesson plans is an essential skill needed by educators. In this class, you will have the opportunity to write a one- to two-page lesson plan for each presentation you are doing. These assignments will help you develop important skills that will serve you in upcoming course work and ultimately your career. You will need to submit your own lesson plan along with a group lesson plan that will reflect the work of all members. Lesson plans will need to include the following:

Learning Outcomes: You will need to identify two to three learning outcomes. What will your classmates be able to think, know, or do as a result of participating in the activity? Identify the level of Bloom's taxonomy that corresponds to each learning outcome.

Learning Activities: List the teaching strategies and activities you plan to use to accomplish the learning outcomes. Include time needed for each strategy or activity.

Assessment: Develop one to two multiple-choice questions and a short answer question for the first presentation and one to two multiple-choice questions for the second presentation. Indicate correct answers for the multiple-choice questions, and include a rubric that you will use to grade the short answer question.

Analytical Rubric: Lesson Plans

Lesson Plans	"D" or "F" Work	"B" or "C" Work	"A" Work
Content	Behavioral terms not used; learning outcomes not clearly explained; little to no connection between outcomes, activities, and assessment questions	Used behavioral terms to identify what students will learn as a result of participating in the lesson; attempted to connect to Bloom's theory; focused on semi-important topics; some connection between learning activities and assessment questions; good use of active learning techniques and research-based practices; rubric lacks specificity	Used behavioral terms to identify what students will learn as a result of participating in the lesson; accurate references to Bloom's taxonomy; focus was on most important points; learning activities and assessment questions were clearly connected to learning outcomes; good use of active learning techniques and research-based practices; rubric would be easy for others to use

Presentations/Teaching Opportunities and Related Written Assignments

Because this is a course that is preparing you to become an educator, doing presentations is important! You will have the opportunity to do two presentations. Although you are working in groups (four to five students) for these learning activities, you are **graded on an individual basis**.

In addition to being an effective presenter of information, you will also need to create clear written documents such as educational lesson plans. Not only will these assignments help you enhance your writing skills, but because they are directly connected to your presentations, they are also designed to help you produce a high-quality presentation.

1. A 10- to 15-minute presentation on an **educational topic** (topic must be approved). Using a PowerPoint as a visual backdrop, you will provide the class with an overview of the research on the topic and practical educational implications. *To maximize the participation of all students in the group and to increase your learning of all the material, you will be assigned parts on the day of the presentation. View this presentation as an individual presentation, but you have a support team.* This assignment includes:

   a. Lesson Plan
   b. Literature Review Paper (Three- to five-page paper done individually; this will help your group function more productively, because everyone will be coming to the table with his or her own contributions!)
   c. PowerPoint Slides
   d. Presentation
   e. Reflection Paper

2. A 30-minute lesson on an assigned article from the **research packet**. This is an opportunity for you to engage the class in significant hands-on learning experiences. Because of the interactive nature of this lesson, your group will get to decide on who will do what task. All members need to have equal parts. This assignment includes:

   a. Lesson Plan
   b. Presentation
   c. Reflection Paper

Literature Review Paper

Developing a strong background knowledge before working with your group members will enable you to make significant contributions to the group discussions. Conducting a literature review and writing a paper on the presentation topic will help you be a productive member of your group and will also assist you with gaining a deeper level of understanding of the material. For this assignment, you will be writing a **three- to five-page paper on your presentation topic**. You will need to find at least seven resources, three of which must be original research studies. The goal is to become knowledgeable about the research in this area. Use the library databases to find peer-reviewed journal articles. In addition to using at least five peer-reviewed journal articles, you can also use research-based books or websites.

Organization of Paper

- *Introduction:* Importance of the topic
- *Three Main Themes That Emerged From the Research:* Include details from at least one original study on each theme
- *Summary:* Review key findings and their importance

Literature Review Analytical Rubric

Paper	"D" or "F" Work	"B" or "C" Work	"A" Work
Content	Inaccurate or minimal information included; lack of organization or flow; did not include original research studies	General overview of the topic; information was accurate but missed some important concepts; difficult to differentiate between main points and supporting details; some details about at least two original studies	Comprehensive overview of the topic; information was accurate and complete; major points were emphasized; good details about at least three original research studies; well organized
Writing Skills	Did not address three main themes; limited to no research support for statements; citations not used or inappropriately used; several spelling and grammatical errors	Good organization: included organization, described three main themes, conclusion summarized key points; most statements supported by research; APA style was used; few spelling and grammatical errors	Well organized: clear introduction, description of approximately three main themes, and strong conclusion; research supported all statements; APA style was used; free of grammatical and spelling errors
Resources	Did not include at least seven scholarly sources; sources were not research based	At least seven scholarly sources were used; some were not research based	At least seven scholarly sources were used; all sources were research based; at least three original studies included

Presentation 1

Topics

1. What Are the Best Practices in Bilingual Education?

2. Is Homework Valuable?

3. Should Children Be Held Back?

4. What Are the Benefits of Extracurricular Activities?

5. What Is the Best Way to Educate Gifted Students?

6. Does Group Work Lead to High Achievement?

7. Does Technology Aid Learning?

8. Should We Lengthen the School Day or Year?

9. What's the Value in Service-Learning?

10. Does Block Scheduling Work?

11. What's the Best Way to Give Feedback When Grading Students?

Task

1. Write a three- to five-page literature review paper (see previous section).
2. Create a lesson plan for this presentation/teaching opportunity (see previous section).
3. Create a PowerPoint presentation to review the literature on your topic. Be sure to include major themes that emerged from the literature, specifics from at least 2 original studies, and educational implications of the research. You will have approximately 10 to 15 minutes for this presentation that consist primarily of direct instruction with 1 or 2 brief opportunities for active learning.
4. Create a visually effective one- to two-page handout for the class that highlights the key points from your presentation. You will post this on Shared Files (you can also distribute it in class if you'd like).
5. Administer the assessment you created; collect responses and grade it (group).
6. Write a brief reflection paper (one page) about your presentation (individual). What went well? What would you do differently next time? Did your assessment results help you know if the learning outcomes were achieved?

Analytical Rubric: Presentation 1

Presenta-tion	"D" or "F" Work	"B" or "C" Work	"A" Work
Content	Inaccurate or minimal information; little to no details on original studies; relied more on opinions versus research	Information was accurate but missed some important concepts; difficult to differentiate between main points and supporting details; minimal information from two original research studies; limited discussion of application	Information was accurate and complete; numerous research findings were discussed and at least two original studies were explained in detail; major points were emphasized and application to education was highlighted
Presentation Style	Read off paper or slides; minimal eye contact; little to no emphasis on main points	Good eye contact and organization of presentation; minimal emphasis on major points so all information seemed equally important	Good eye contact and engagement; well organized: major points were emphasized; brief active learning techniques helped students learn material
PowerPoint Presentation and Handout	Relied solely or almost solely on the use of words with little organizational structure; not enough information or too much information on slides	Some use of organizational strategies such as bullets, but limited use of tools such as SmartArt, graphs, or tables	Information presented in very clear and well-organized fashion; effective use of SmartArt, graphs, tables, and so on. to visually organize the information; amount of information provided was substantial but not overwhelming
Time Management	Did not follow the time plan	Generally on target with time but some activities took more or less time than planned	All activities were completed within the allotted time

Presentation 2

Presentation 1 Article Choices

1. APA- Zero tolerance policies (2008): **Behavior Management**

2. Recht and Leslie (1998): **Reading Comprehension**

3. Schwartz, Son, Kornell, and Finn (2011): **Memory**

4. Clark, Kircshner, and Sweller (2012): **Fully Guided Instruction**

5. Wlodkowski (1999): **Motivation**

Task

1. Create a lesson plan for this presentation/teaching opportunity (submitted previously).
2. Engage the class in a 20- to 30-minute active learning lesson on your article (group). Your role is to facilitate learning through active learning exercises.
3. Administer the assessment you created; collect responses (group).
4. Grade the assessment (individual, group). Submit a grading summary sheet that includes the average overall grade (mean) and average score for each question (including short answer).
5. Write a brief reflection paper (one page) about your presentation (individual). What went well? What would you do differently next time? Did your assessment results help you know if the learning outcomes were achieved? What worked well and what did not in terms of your rubric?

Analytical Rubric: Presentation 2

Presentation	"D" or "F" Work	"B" or "C" Work	"A" Work
Content	Inaccurate or minimal information from the article	Information was accurate but missed some important concepts; difficult to differentiate between main points and supporting details	Information was accurate and complete; major points were emphasized
Active Learning Activity: Directions and Monitoring	Directions unclear; students confused about what to do; answers to questions were not helpful; limited amount of monitoring	General overview of activity provided but some confusion emerged; moved around the room and provided some additional guidance as needed	Directions were shared verbally and in writing and were clearly articulated; answered questions well; moved around the room to be sure students were on track with activity
Active Learning Activity: Appropriateness to Task	The activity did not help students master the content from the article	The activity helped students grasp content from the article but did not emphasize major points	The activity helped students master the content with emphasis on main points from article
Time Management	Did not follow the time plan	Generally on target with time but some activities took more or less time than planned	All activities were completed within the allotted time
Engagement	Facilitators exhibited low levels of energy, and students did not appear to be engaged	Some energy was exhibited by facilitators, and most students were attentive and engaged	Facilitators were enthusiastic about the activity, and students were highly engaged throughout the activity

Reflection Papers

Reflecting on your work is an excellent way to improve your performance. After each presentation, you will be writing a one- to two-page reflection paper. In this paper, you will discuss what went well and what improvements you plan to make the next time you present. Be specific and use educational terminology. You will need to include the grading information from the mini assessment you gave at the end of your presentation. Please submit this online in our learning management system.

Analytical Rubric: Reflection Paper

Lesson Plans	"D" or "F" Work	"B" or "C" Work	"A" Work
Content	Vague, general comments about presentation made; did not include grading information	General comments about what worked and what didn't; lacking specifics about how to improve; grading information included	Specific information about what did. and did not go well with the presentation; several specific strategies (with reference to educational terminology) were identified for improving the next presentation; focus on learning and details about grading included

Quizzes

Practicing retrieval is a very effective learning strategy. In fact, researchers have found that testing yourself is one of the best ways to learn (Roediger & Karpicke, 2006). To maximize your learning experience, you will be taking a quiz on every chapter. Quizzes are online. You can take each quiz up to three times (lots of retrieval practice!), and the highest score will count. These are called formative assessments—they are designed to help you learn.

The first quiz is on Academic Integrity. To help you avoid unintentional dishonesty, all students are expected to view the Academic Integrity Narrated PowerPoint presentation (link also in the learning management system) and take a 25-question online quiz. You can take the quiz as many times as necessary but will need to achieve 100% (scores lower than 100% will be changed to 0%).

Exams

You will take a midterm and final exam, composed of short answer questions from the reading assignments. This is a great opportunity for you to "show what you know" and celebrate all you've learned. These are called summative assessments, showing the "sum" of all of your learning! However, there are many learning benefits associated with reflecting on your performance after the exam.

Reading Assignments/Final Exam Review Sheet

To accomplish all of our learning goals, you will need to be engaged in lots of learning outside of the classroom. You will be expected to read the text and articles. To help you actively engage with the text, you will be completing reading assignments, typing answers to the questions posed. While we will be reviewing some of the concepts from the text in class, we will simply not have enough time to cover everything. As you are a future educator, all of the information is important! Your exams will be composed of your reading assignment questions.

Examples of Chapter Reading Assignment Questions

Chapter 1

1. What theories are associated with Erikson, Pavlov, Skinner, Bandura, Piaget, and Vygotsky?
2. What impact does the teacher–student relationship have on academic performance?
3. What is the experimental research method? Why can we say causation with this model? What are independent, dependent, and confounding variables?
4. What is the correlational research method? What can we say about the results found using this method? What correlation would indicate a strong relationship? What is the difference between a positive correlation and a negative correlation?

5. What are some ethical problems that can arise when doing research? How can we address these problems?
6. What are the key components of an effective teacher mind-set according to Brooks?

Chapter 14

1. Who is Bloom? Describe his taxonomy of learning. What changes were made to his taxonomy in 2001?
2. According to research, what are the pros and cons of homework? What are the best ways to use seatwork and homework?
3. What was the key finding from the Rosenthal and Jacobson study on the Pygmalian effect?
4. What do expert teachers do? How does this differ from novice teachers?
5. What should drive the creation of a lesson plan? What are the key components of a lesson plan?
6. What are advance organizers? What strategies can teachers use to ask effective questions?
7. What is differentiated instruction?

References

American Psychological Association Zero Tolerance Task Force. (2008). Are zero tolerance policies effective in the schools? An evidentiary review and recommendations. *American Psychologist, 63*(9), 852–862.

Clark, R. E., Kircshner, P. A., & Sweller, J. (2012). Putting students on the path to learning: The case for fully guided instruction. *American Educator*, 6–11.

Dickinson, D. J., & O'Connell, D. Q. (1990). Effect of quality and quantity of study on student grades. *Journal of Educational Research, 83*(4), 227.

Gadzella, B., & Baloglu, M. (2003). High and low achieving education students on processing, retaining, and retrieval of information. *Journal of Instructional Psychology, 30*(2), 99. Retrieved from Academic Search Premier database.

Goswami, U. (2008). Principles of learning, implications for teaching: A cognitive neuroscience perspective. *Journal of Philosophy of Education, 42*(3–4), 381–399.

Hogan, T., Rabinowitz, M., & Craven, J. A. (2003). Representation in teaching: Inferences from research on expert and novice teachers. *Educational Psychologist, 38*(4), 235–247.

Kiewra, K., DuBois, N., Christian, D., McShane, A., Meyerhof-fer, M., & Roskelley, D. (1991). Note-taking functions and tech-niques. *Journal of Educational Psychology*, *83*(2), 240–245. doi:10.1037/0022-0663.83.2.240

Krathwohl, D. R., & Anderson, L. W. (2010). Merlin C. Wittrock and the revision of Bloom's taxonomy. *Educational Psychologist*, *45*(1), 64–65.

Mayer, R. E. (2009). *Multimedia learning* (2nd ed.). New York, NY: Cambridge University Press.

McDaniel, M. A., Howard, D. C., & Einstein, G. O. (2009). The read-recite-review study strategy: Effective and portable. *Psychological Science*, *20*(4), 516–522. doi:10.1111/j.1467-9280.2009.02325.x

McGuire, S. Y. (2015). *Teach students how to learn: Strategies you can incorporate into any course to improve student metacognition, study skills, and motivation*. Sterling, VA: Stylus.

National Reading Panel. (2000). *Teaching children to read: An evidence-based assess-ment of the scientific research literature on reading and its implications for reading instruction*. Washington, DC: National Institute of Child Health and Human Development, National Institutes of Health.

Ramstetter, C. L., Murray, R., & Garner, A. S. (2010). The crucial role of recess in schools. *Journal of School Health*, *80*(11), 517–526.

Recht, D. R., & Leslie, L. (1988). Effect of prior knowledge on good and poor readers' memory of text. *Journal of Educational Psychology*, *80*(1), 16–20. doi:10.1037/00220663.80.1.16

Roediger, H., & Karpicke, J. D. (2006). Test-enhanced learning: Taking mem-ory tests improves long-term retention. *Psychological Science*, *17*(3), 249–255. doi:10.1111/j.1467-9280.2006.01693.x

Schwartz, B. L., Son, L. K., Kornell, N., & Finn, B. (2011). Four principles of memory improvement: A guide to improving learning efficiency. *The Interna-tional Journal of Creativity and Problem Solving*, *21*(1), 7–15.

Strage, A., Baba, Y., Millner, S., Scharberg, M., Walker, E., Williamson, R., & Yoder, M. (2002). What every student affairs professional should know: Student study activities and beliefs associated with academic success. *Journal of College Student Development*, *43*(2), 246–266. Retrieved from PsycINFO database.

Walker, I., & Crogan, M. (1998). Academic performance, prejudice, and the Jigsaw Classroom: New pieces to the puzzle. *Journal of Community and Applied Social Psychology*, *8*(6), 381–393.

Wlodkowski, R. J. (1999). Motivation and diversity: A framework for teaching. *New Directions for Teaching and Learning*, *78*(1), 7–16.

Zimmerman, B. J., & DiBenedetto, M. K. (2008). Mastery learning and assessment: Implications for students and teachers in an era of high-stakes testing. *Psychology in the Schools*, *45*(3), 206–216. doi:10.1002/pits.20291

ABOUT THE AUTHORS

Christine Harrington has been a faculty member at Middlesex County College for almost 20 years, serving as the director of the Center for the Enrichment of Learning and Teaching (CELT) for 5 of these years. She is currently serving a 2-year term as the executive director of the New Jersey Center for Student Success at the New Jersey Council of County Colleges. Upon completing this term, she will head back into the classroom, teaching psychology and student success courses. Harrington also teaches graduate courses in learning and teaching at Rutgers University. She is the author of a research-based textbook for first-year seminars, *Student Success in College: Doing What Works!* (3rd edition; Wadsworth Publishing, 2018), and *Dynamic Lecturing: Research-Based Strategies to Enhance Lecture Effectiveness* (with Todd Zakrajsek as a coauthor; Stylus, 2017). She was the 2016 recipient of the Excellence in Teaching First-Year Experience award, presented at the Annual Conference on the First-Year Experience. Harrington is frequently invited to give plenary speeches at national teaching and learning conferences, such as the Lilly Conference Series on College and University Teaching and Learning and the Annual Conference on the First-Year Experience, as well as colleges and universities across the nation.

Melissa Thomas is a lecturer for the College of Natural Sciences at the University of Texas at Austin for the Texas Interdisciplinary Plan (TIP) Scholars program, a wraparound program for potentially at-risk students. Since 1999, TIP has sought to provide a small college experience for over 450 first-year students in the College of Liberal Arts and the College of Natural Sciences. The program provides academic and social support through smaller classes, academic advising, linked courses, a critical thinking seminar, social connections, academic peer mentoring, and academic tutoring. Previously, she was the director of the Center for Student Learning at the College of Charleston, where she provided leadership and management to all the programs and service provided to students by the center. Before that, Thomas was an adjunct instructor, common reads selection committee member at two institutions, principal investigator for a multiyear grant, coordinator of a graduate student academic support program, and past president of the College Reading and Learning Association. Through her work on various common intellectual experiences (CIEs) and other high-impact practices, her research interests include common read programs, motivation inside and outside the classroom, critical thinking in action, group communication, assessment, and student success. Thomas holds a juris doctorate from the University of Texas at Austin and a bachelor of arts degree in communication from the University of Texas at San Antonio.

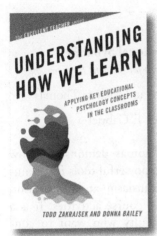

Understanding How We Learn

Applying Key Educational Psychology Concepts in the Classroom

Todd Zakrajsek and Donna Bailey

This succinct, jargon-free, and user-friendly volume offers faculty an introduction to 35 concepts from educational psychology that illuminate what's going through the minds of learners as they grapple with new information.

The concepts are conveniently grouped under major topics, each introduced by a summary of the field, its origins, the latest relevant research, and the implications for teaching: cognition and thinking, memory, learning, perceiving and living in the world, working in groups, motivation, and perceptions of self.

Within each section Todd Zakrajsek and Donna Bailey provide summaries of each key concept. They explain the terminology, its background, and relevance to student learning and offer ideas and tips for immediate application in teaching.

This is an illuminating book for teachers seeking to understand student learning, offering a foundational understanding of educational terms often tossed about in discussions of student learning and a range of solutions to challenges they commonly encounter in the classroom.

Sty/us

22883 Quicksilver Drive
Sterling, VA 20166-2019 Subscribe to our e-mail alerts: www.Styluspub.com

Also in the Excellent Teacher series

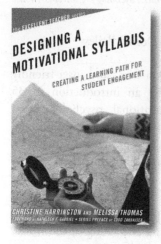

Designing a Motivational Syllabus
Creating a Learning Path for Student Engagement

Christine Harrington and Melissa Thomas

Foreword by Kathleen F. Gabriel

"Harrington and Thomas demonstrate how course syllabi can be powerful tools for stimulating students' enthusiasm and motivation to actively engage in course activities. It is a must-read for all faculty who want to construct a syllabus that is sure to increase student engagement and learning!"—*Saundra McGuire, Director Emerita, Center for Academic Success, Louisiana State University*

"This book is a useful guide for improving an existing syllabus or designing a new one. Harrington and Thomas demonstrate how a syllabus is much more than an informative document—they show us how it can be a valuable tool to motivate students and assist them in their learning."—*Kathleen F. Gabriel, School of Education; California State University, Chico*

"Harrington and Thomas provide compelling rationale and evidence for why instructors would want to reimagine their syllabus, while offering practical advice for how to create a document that accurately articulates their vision, motivates students, and fosters learning. Instructors, whether wishing to make small changes to their syllabi or to totally rethink the why and hows of their courses, will find this book an invaluable resource."—*Michael Palmer, Director, Center for Teaching Excellence, University of Virginia*

"Presents new ways of thinking about the role of the syllabus. Drawing from current research on best practices, Harrington and Thomas provide thorough context and make a strong case for an effective course syllabus as a foundational tool to shape student learning. This book will undoubtedly be valuable to new and experienced teachers as well as faculty development professionals."—*Billie Bennett Franchini, Institute for Teaching, Learning and Academic Leadership, SUNY Albany*

(Continues on preceeding page)